purestyle

purestyle

Jane Cumberbatch
photography by **Henry Bourne**

RYLAND
PETERS
& SMALL
LONDON NEW YORK

For this edition
Designer **Sarah Fraser**
Editor **Miriam Hyslop**
Picture Research **Tracy Ogino**
Production Manager **Patricia Harrington**
Art Director **Gabriella Le Grazie**
Publishing Director **Alison Starling**

First published in
the United States in 1996,
this edition first published in 2005 by
Ryland Peters & Small, Inc.
519 Broadway
5th Floor
New York NY10012
www.rylandpeters.com

10 9 8 7 6 5 4 3 2 1

Text © Jane Cumberbatch 1996, 2005
Design and photographs copyright © Ryland
Peters & Small 1996, 2005

Library of Congress Cataloging-in-Publication Data

Cumberbatch, Jane.
  Pure style / Jane Cumberbatch ; photography by
Henry Bourne.-- 2nd ed.
      p. cm.
  Includes index.
  ISBN 1-84172-865-9
  1. Interior decoration. I. Title: Pure style. II. Bourne,
Henry. III.
Title.
  NK2115.C975 2005
  747--dc22

                                           2004016484

contents

Introduction   6

Elements   10
Color   12
Texture   26
Scent and Taste   32
Fabrics   36
Furniture   44
Objects   52
Putting it all Together   64
Culinary Living   66
Relaxed Living   86
Sleeping in Style   102
Clean Living   114
Outdoor Living   126

Credits   132
Suppliers   134
Index   140
Acknowledgments   144

introduction

Pure Style is not just about rooms and furnishings, or about trying to create an impossibly perfect glossy lifestyle. *Pure Style* is about trying to create a balance. It's about making life luxurious, not in a costly, glitzy sense, but in a more matter-of-fact, practical and natural way. *Pure Style* is about paring down and trying to live with less clutter (the fewer things we have to fuss about, the more we can get on with living). It's about simple, basic design that combines function and beauty of form to create a look that is crisp, clean, classic, and timeless.

Pure Style: Innovative ideas for crisp, clean, contemporary living.

pure style

Pure Style is about being economical
without skimping on essential things
like good food or a decent bed.

Pure Style is not concerned with slavishly
following fashions in interiors; it's about being practical and
resourceful—tracking down great domestic staples that have
been around a long time, using the high street chain stores for
good basic buys, or seeking out secondhand furniture that can
be revitalized with a coat of paint. *Pure Style* focuses on the
sensual side of living: such as texture—sudsy soap, rough log
baskets, string bags, a twiggy wreath entwined with fresh
rosemary sprigs, or the bliss of sleeping in pure white cotton
sheets; scents—fresh flowers, scented candles, or laundry aired
outside in the hot sun; tastes—good bread or new potatoes
cooked with fresh mint; color—light, bright, airy, matte shades
inspired by nature as found in Queen Anne's Lace, egg and calico
whites, butter and straw yellows, bean greens, sea and sky
blues, and earth tones; natural things—moss,
lichen, shells, pebbles; smells—great
coffee, chocolate, and delicious
wine; fabrics—good value,
durable, and decorative, in simple
patterns like checks and stripes;
basics—functional items that look good,
such as a tin mug, a pudding basin, or glass mason jars.

Pure Style is about creating living, breathing spaces throughout the house. This book shows you how to be functional and practical in the kitchen, with durable counters, proper cupboards, and the essential kitchen utensils. *Pure Style* is about making the rituals of eating as sensual as is practical or possible and shows how simple elements—white plates, starched linen, and jars of cut flowers—can create pleasing and visually satisfying table arrangements. *Pure Style* also demonstrates how plain but delicious basic ingredients—good cheese, fresh fish, best quality fruit and vegetables—are the key to hassle-free food preparation. For the sitting room, *Pure Style* illustrates how a combination of elements and textures, such as comfortable seating, beautiful fabrics in cotton, wool, and muslin, and candlelight and blazing fires, help to make a room relaxing and peaceful. To help you slumber more soundly, *Pure Style* shows you the benefits of well-made beds and proper mattresses as well as the luscious qualities of crisp cotton bedlinen, snuggly warm woollen blankets, and quilts. For the bathroom, this book demonstrates how lots of piping hot water, together with soft cotton towels and wonderful soaps, make bathing a truly pleasurable experience.

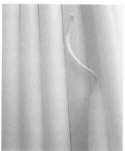

elements

To touch, to hold, to look, to smell, to taste: the sensual aspects of life are there to be nurtured and enjoyed. Engage the senses and explore the visceral elements around you. Douse your sensibilities with tactile elements: incorporate inspiring colors and textures into your home to make life an altogether more spirited and rewarding affair.

color

Use color to make daily living more pleasurable and
uplifting. Thinking about how color appears in
nature gives clues to choosing the sorts of colors you
might want to have in your home. Neutrals are
timeless and easy to live with, while white is
unifying, restful, and a favorite with those who seek
a simple approach to living. Greens are versatile,
ranging from the brightest lime to much subtler
tones, and earthy hues of brown can be used for a
variety of looks. The sea and sky colors found in
denim, on china, bedlinen, and in paint give clarity
and crispness to interior settings. Look at garden
borders to appreciate the range of pinks and transfer
these indoors as soft lilac walls or muted floral
cottons. Creams and yellows are cheerful, optimistic
colors and have universal appeal. *Pure Style* is not
about slavishly coordinated color schemes, although
it does show you how to put together rooms and
interiors with accents on color. It is more about
considering the colors around us and incorporating
them into our daily lives. Color is a vital element in
characterizing an interior and it need not be
expensive. If you cannot afford a complete
redecoration, subtly change the emphasis with
different pillows, covers, and splashes of floral detail.

whites

Milk

Egg white

Wax white

Bone

Oatmeal

Muslin

Brilliant white, eggshell white, bone white, limestone white, and even plain old white, are just some examples of the plethora of available contrasting white hues and tones. White creates a peaceful and timeless ambience that benefits both period and starker contemporary settings. It is a minimalist's dream shade and makes for harmonious, unifying spaces. In today's super-charged, technical world it's good for the soul to retreat into a reviving white oasis where simplicity rules. For an all-white scheme, strip and then paint floorboards in white floor paint and seal with a yacht varnish; use white emulsion on the walls and ceilings. So that the whole interior does not look too much like the inside of a refrigerator, create tonal contrasts by giving the woodwork hints of off-white, bone, or white with gray. For a unifying effect, paint furniture in similar shades and add cotton drill slip-on covers, muslin pillows, and diaphanous gauze drapes. Complete the look with accessories such as white china and bedlinen.

Washed blue

Sea

Beach-hut blue

Denim

Checked blue

blues

Blue spans a host of color variations, from deep hyacinth to very pale ice-blue. It can turn to lavender when mixed with violet, and turquoise when blended with green. In the middle of the spectrum are the purer blues of bachelor's buttons and bright powder blue. Take a cue from the fashion world and look at the soft blues that characterize denim as it is washed and worn. These shades adapt as easily to home furnishings as they do to jeans and jackets. Pale shades are the tones most likely to appear cold, especially in north-facing rooms. The trick here is to use warming devices, such as faded kelims or terra-cotta flowerpots, perhaps in a room with duck-egg blue walls. If a pure blue is too strong for your taste, try a duller mix of gray, green, and blue. This works well with highlights of white: try a dining room scheme in a subdued blue, offset with white-painted furniture, blue-and-white check curtains, and bowls of white narcissi. For a more homespun look, combine the muted Shaker blues with red-and-white striped or checked cotton.

Useful decorating details in blue include tartan china and clear blue glass. There is blue-and-white ticking for loose covers and storage bags. For a jaunty beach-house theme, make up chair covers in bright lavender blue, cricket-stripe cotton, and faded blue-jean cotton pillows (various denim weights are available from fabric wholesalers).

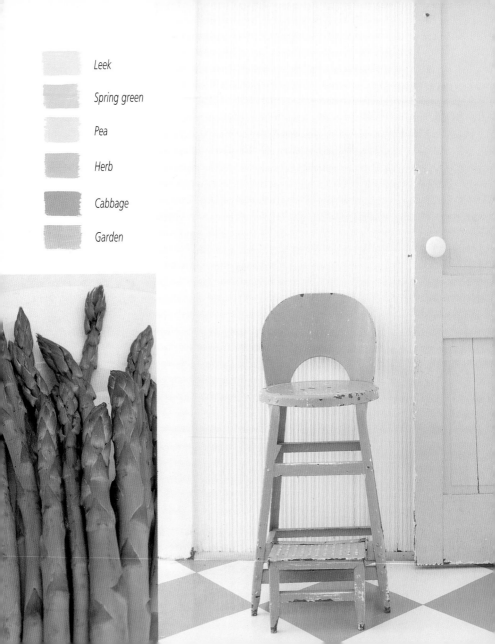

Leek

Spring green

Pea

Herb

Cabbage

Garden

green

Green is one of the most accommodating colors for interiors. In a contemporary setting a vivid apple-green or lime teamed with flourishes of fuchsia pink can work well, while traditional interiors call for duller shades mixed with gray, such as hopsack and olive. Take inspiration from the range of greens in nature; look at the lime-green stems of hyacinths or the blades of fresh spring grass. Peas in their pods and cabbage leaves provide another source of

vibrant and sometimes variegated greens. Try using sage-and-white striped cotton for chair covers with bursts of lime green for pillows.

pink and lavender

Pink does not need to be a sickly color associated with frilly, little-girl bedrooms, over-the-top chintzy floral drawing rooms, or the monotonous peach-colored bathrooms that are perennial in mass-produced home design catalogs. At the other extreme, shocking-pink walls and ceilings are hardly a recipe for subtle, understated living. Careful selection and combinations of pinks with other colors are therefore the key to making a stylish, comfortable statement. In contemporary settings, fuchsia pink, lavender, and green combine well—just look to the flowerbeds outside for inspiration and think of purple lavender heads on sage-green foliage or foxglove bells with bright green stalks and leaves. For a stylish, modern scheme for a living room paint the walls white, cover the chairs in pale lavender, and make up pillows in plain fuchsia and lime-green cottons. Hot pink floral prints look great married to white walls and white slipcovers, creating a fresh, crisp look. More delicate pink schemes need careful consideration to avoid looking bland. For a pink, though not at all prissy bedroom, paint walls a warm shade such as a pale rose with a hint of brown and furnish the

 Hyacinth

 Foxglove

Lavender

Marshmallow

Lilac

room with a lavender-colored antique patchwork quilt and muslin Roman blinds—the whole effect will be clean and subtle with the added touch of color. On the culinary front, think of enticing, deep pink, fresh strawberry ice cream; sticky and spongy marshmallows and violet-cream candies. Less threatening to body shape are pink turnips, rhubarb, radiccio leaves, and even pink pasta. For bright detail try adding smooth plastic objects in pink, such as mugs, brushes, and buckets.

earth and terra-cotta

Because earthy hues are universally adaptable base colors it is hard to go wrong with them, except for those really drab, mud-colored schemes that were so popular during the Seventies. Ranging from dark chocolate to cream, brown accents work well in both rustic and contemporary settings. Consider the terra-cotta-colored façades that are prevalent throughout Provençe and Spain, the brown woodwork and detailing of an English cottage kitchen, or the terra-cotta flagstones and wooden beams in a New England farmhouse. In contrast, imagine a white, utilitarian, urban loft with schoolhouse-style, dark wooden desks, tables, chairs, and filing cabinets. Study the shades of soil, from a clay-based red to a rich, dark brown, and see how they act as a foil for brighter colors in nature. Clay pots

are perfect for setting off the foliage and flowers of emerging spring bulbs. Be bold with earthy tones. For instance, paint a dining room in a rich Etruscan shade for a warm effect both night and day. Even boring beige is still a favorite shade and fabric companies love it for its versatility. Beige looks smart in various clever contemporary reworkings such as coir and natural fiber matting for floors, tough neutral linen for curtains and chair covers, or brown office files and filing boxes. Use striped and checked cotton in pinkish terra-cotta and white to give chair covers and curtains a wonderfully natural feel.

Chocolate

Sack

Coir

Clay

Brick

yellow

Creamy yellows, reminiscent of the countryside, are wonderfully adaptable and increase the sense of space in cramped and darkened rooms. When decorating, opt for the softer end of the yellow spectrum as acidic yellows are harder to live with because of their sharpness. However, do not go too

pale, as at the other end of the scale, very clear, light primrose shades can appear insipid. Creams and yellows look great with white or even orange. Some shades look much darker in the paint can, but once on the walls are wonderfully rich and very well-suited to period hallways and kitchens. A slightly more acidic yellow will be lighter yet still rich in color and should look good in artificial light and really glowing when the sun shines. There are also some very rich, bright yellows available. If you can withstand their intensity, these strong shades will illuminate and cheer up even the smallest spaces and look fabulous against blue-and-white china and furnishings. Cream or yellow paint looks good on walls and as a decorative color for furniture. In a cream-colored kitchen, choose traditional stone bowls and white dishes to suit the simple theme. In living rooms, yellow walls look good against mustard-colored checked and plain cottons, with contrasting details in terra-cotta or blue. Yellows really come into their own in springtime when rooms are filled with daffodils and other flowers.

Butter

Honey

Pudding basin

Straw

Mustard

texture

Scant attention is paid to our senses by the purveyors of today's technological gadgetry with their ever-increasing obsession for convenience and labor-saving devices. There is not much textural appeal, for example, about computer hardware, or mass-produced, static-inducing synthetic carpets and fabrics. In complete contrast, sensual textures like soft wool blankets, crisp cotton bedlinens, and light and downy pillows are staples handed down from past generations that help to bolster us against the more soulless elements of modern living. From the perfect smoothness of a baby's skin to the gnarled and ridged bark on a tree, natural textures are there for us to notice and appreciate. They often combine an alluring mix of qualities. For instance, lumps of volcanic pumice stone, logs, and shells are defined as rough or smooth, depending on the degree of erosion upon them by wind, sun, fire, and rain. It is this very naturalness that compels us to gather such things for the house. Our homes need natural textures to transform them into living breathing spaces. Polished wooden floors, rough log baskets, and pure cotton fabrics are just some of the organic items that we can introduce to suggest this enriching effect.

smooth

Smooth objects are often fresh and clean and appear all around the house, especially in the kitchen and bathroom. Washing activities spring to mind, such as a handful of foaming soap or a big plastic bucketful of hot soapy water. The satisfyingly smooth surfaces of white tiling and marble or utilitarian stainless steel conjure up a sense of clinical, streamlined efficiency. In kitchens, culinary preparation is made more efficient and hygienic when work surfaces can easily be rinsed, wiped, and made pristine. Utensils such as sparkling stainless-steel pots and pans also help to keep culinary tasks running smoothly. I love to cook with a selection of worn wooden spoons which have somehow molded to my grip after years of devoted use. Smooth, cast-iron bathtub surfaces and ceramic tiled walls can be scoured and scrubbed so helping to keep bathrooms squeaky clean. Indoors as well as out, natural surfaces such as slate or well-worn flags are texturally pleasing. Smooth elements exist in a diversity of guises, from soft white tissue paper tied up with silk ribbon to polished floorboards. On the theme of food, smooth goodies include wonderfully slippery waxed paper that gourmet

shops wrap cheese in, slender glass bottles of
olive oil, or slivers of fine chocolate in layers of
the thinnest silver paper. You can bring naturally
smooth objects indoors for textural decoration,
such as ancient weathered pebbles and scoured
driftwood picked up on a beach hunt.

rough

One of my favorite possessions is a roughly hewn,
olivewood basket from Spain. Made from the winter
prunings of olive trees it is silvery-gray in color, robust
in design, and a sheer pleasure to touch and hold. The
locals in Spain use such baskets to transport eggs, wild
mushrooms, oranges, or tomatoes from their vegetable
patches, while mine is filled with kindling for the fireplace.
Rough, tough, and hairy flooring in sisal and coir is
durable and, even when woven into patterns, it still looks
like a natural texture.

Equally, a rough terra cotta-tiled floor is not only
satisfying to walk on but also has the appearance of
having been in place forever if its tiles are not laid in
exact uniformity. Rough textures in nature have usually
been created by the elements, and even sun-blistered paint,

(a painter and decorators nightmare,) can create a visually pleasing finish on a weathered old shed. This sense of roughness allied to age means that unevenly plastered or whitewashed walls or features such as battered tongue-and-groove paneled doors can make even a new house look rustic. Rough can mean contemporary too, and utilitarian concrete walls and floors are common features in industrial buildings converted into open, loft-style living spaces.

Roughness is not always a pleasing texture, as anyone with chapped hands or prickly wool next to the skin knows, yet some fabrics such as cotton towels worn rough by repeated washing are perfect for an exhilarating rubdown after a shower. Tools such as pumice stones and hard bristle brushes assist exfoliation and improve circulation.

scent and taste

Scents and tastes are so evocative that childhood memories may be unexpectedly recalled by a certain waft of perfume or the aroma of a particular food. As a small girl on vacation in continental hotels, I invariably associated France with a cocktail of scents that included furniture polish, smelly plumbing, and cooked garlic. In the same way, the first sweet grass clippings of spring, evident as I pass by a newly mown park or suburban backyard, transport me back to games played on the lawn at my grandmother's house in the country. Smells quicken our senses, increase anticipation, and act as powerful stimuli— there is nothing like the whiff of strong coffee and toast to entice slothful risers out of bed. Taste is crucial to the pleasure we take in eating. In addition to a knowledge and appreciation of basic cooking skills, fresh ingredients are vital if food is to taste good. There is a world of difference between a homemade hamburger and the creations served at fast-food chains. Smell and taste are closely related, and one without the other would diminish the intensity of many eating experiences. Consider the first strawberry of the summer; its heady, flowery scent is a beguiling hint of the sweetness that is to follow.

flavor and fragrance

It is invigorating to have good smells around the house. I love paper-white narcissi, whose flowers emit the most delicious sweet smell. Scented candles and bowls of potpourri are other sources of floral scents. In the kitchen, scents and tastes come to the fore: the fragrant citrus tang of grated lemon peel accompanies the preparation of sauces and desserts and the earthy scent of wild mushrooms being fried rapidly in butter is any food lovers idea of heaven. Simple tastes are often the most sublime. What could be more enticing than a bowl of pasta mixed with garlic and a little olive oil, or a good, strong cheese? Herbs such as basil, rosemary, thyme, and dill smell delicious and help to draw out the flavors of food.

fabrics

Setting taste and aesthetic considerations aside, the criteria for choosing one type of furnishing fabric over another include the suitability of the weight and weave for a particular type of furnishing and the fabrics ability to withstand the effects of everyday wear and tear. Cotton, linen, wool, silk, synthetic, and mixed fibers for furnishing exist in a wealth of colors, textures, and weights, and with a little effort it should be possible to find just about anything you want at a price you can afford. If you fall for a really expensive fabric that is over your budget, invest in a small amount for a pillow or two instead. Otherwise, its worth hunting around at a sale for the larger quantities needed for upholstery. For good value basics, go to an old-fashioned fabric store and track down companies who supply the television, film, theater, and art trades. These are great places to find varied weights of muslin, such as those used for toiles in the fashion business, or extra-wide widths of canvas used as stage backdrops and cheap rolls of gauze employed by designers for sets and costumes. One popular silk specialist I know carries a vast stock of colored silks, including parachute silk. In the next six pages, you will find dozens of examples of utility fabrics.

light

Lighter-weight fabrics are brilliant for simple, filmy window treatments. Make decorative half-drapes from voile or gauze (see 24 and 27) panels with cased headings. Thread them onto narrow rods and anchor them within the window frame. Other light-weight drape ideas include unlined cotton (see 6, 7, 8) or linen (see 22) drops with tapes or ribbon loops at the top. Basic roller blinds in fine fabrics (see 9) look subtle and understated in a cream or white decoration scheme. Perfect for bedrooms and bathrooms are filmy transparent loose covers in voile (see 12) for chairs with pretty, curvy shapes. Soft Indian cotton in bright lime green (see 26) and other hot up-to-the-minute shades are great for making up colorful and inexpensive throw-pillow covers. If you're in the mood, sew your own sheets, duvet covers, and pillowcases in cotton sheeting (see 1), which comes in very wide widths. Covers should fit loosely around a duvet and have a generous opening secured with buttons, velcro, or simple ties to make them easy to slip on and off. Printed cotton lawn dress fabric is also worth considering for sprigged floral pillow cases and throw-pillow covers. Cotton sheeting is also a great staple for lightweight tablecloths and napkins.

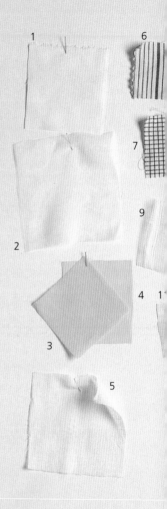

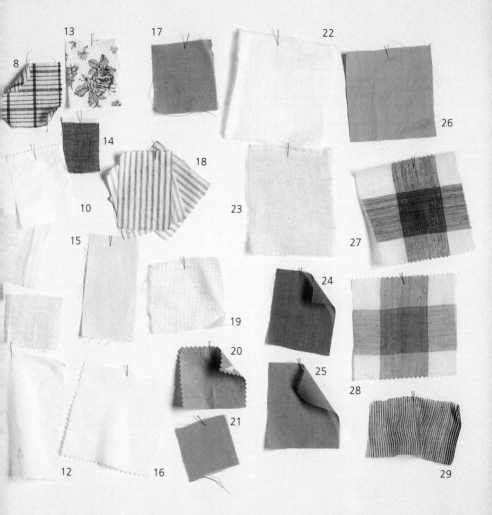

For details of the fabrics shown on pages 38–43 see pages 132–133

30

31

32

33

34

35

36

37

38

39

40

41

42

43

44

45

46

47

48

49

50

51

52

53

54

55

56

57

58

61

versatile

60

63

65

59

I have a passion for blue-checked cotton (see 34 and 60) and use it all around the house for crisp color and detail; as throw pillows (see 58 and 59) for assorted chairs and as Roman drapes (see 34 and 59) in the dining and sitting room. Blue checked slipcovers also look good, and can be as basic or as decorative as you want—with bows, piping, ties, or button detailing, simple pleats, short skirts, or flowing hemlines. Window-seat pillows in cream linen with a piped trim are smart, and this fabric also works well as an idea for covers on daybed bolster pillows. If the fabric is not shrink resistant, and covers are to be washed rather than dry-cleaned, pre-wash all materials including piping before making. Blue-and-white striped cotton, a robust cotton twill closely woven in narrow stripes and traditionally used for pillows and mattress covers, is also another favorite (see 45) and looks especially good as simple drapes with ties at my attic windows, and across an alcove that houses children's clothes. Ticking is also an attractive, classic idea for chair and sofa covers. Continuing on a striped theme, an all-time favorite is a lightweight lavender-blue-and-white printed cotton (see 47) that I've used for tablecloths and chair covers for summer suppers out in the garden.

durable

Tough all-purpose fabrics include canvas (see 82 and 83), sometimes known as duck, that is great for garden chairs and awnings. It's also good for Roman drapes and bolster covers. Cream-colored muslin is one of the best fabrics ever invented—it's incredibly cheap but manages to look smart and understated, and is durable, washable, and perfectly practical. Calico comes in a number of weights; the finer qualities are more appropriate for slipcovers or throw pillow, while thicker weights work well as blinds or drapes (see 75). Tough cotton denim (see 69) looks good on chairs after it's been put through several very hot washes to fade its dark indigo color. For a crisp, tailored look, chairs demand tight coverings to emphasize their shape. A self-patterned herby green cotton and viscose with simple tulips is one of my favorite upholstery fabrics (see 87), and it looks great on one of my secondhand armchairs. Sofas with a contemporary feel look wonderful in solid sea-green and blue colors in tightly woven cottons (see 88, 89, 90). Alternatively, plain cream cotton is stylish, but choose some slightly more forgiving muddy-colored linen if you have a family. Wool tartan (see 79) is another smart idea for upholstering the seats of dining chairs or sofas.

69 74

68

70

75

71 72

73

fabrics

42

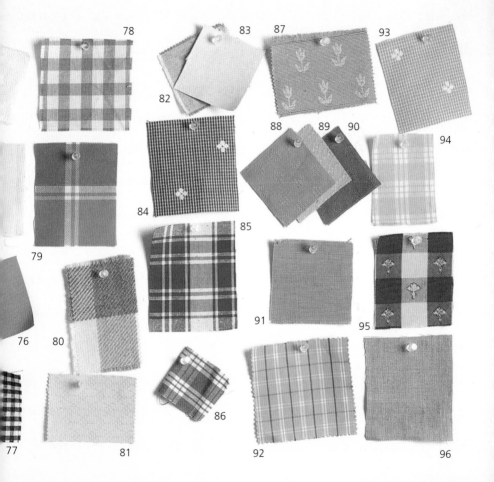

78

83

87

93

82

84

88 89 90

94

79

85

91

95

76 80

86

77 81 92 96

furniture

It may seem paradoxical, but I think that a diversity of objects can imbue an interior with a sense of character and uniformity. Old, new, decorative, industrial, contemporary, or utilitarian, it's possible to combine a variety of furniture styles under one roof and yet create a strong visual statement. Fashion pundits and supermodels dictate the length of hemlines from season to season, but thankfully, trends in interiors are less mercurial. Nevertheless, it is worth putting the same energies into assembling a look for your home as you would for your wardrobe. As with desirable outfits, buy your furniture only after considering texture, comfort, shape, and form. At home, I have gathered together items of furniture obtained from sales, secondhand stores, and family—everything from 18th-century oak dining chairs and old sofas to fold-up tables, painted junk filing cabinets, and kitchen chairs. My only proviso has been to weed out or revamp anything that I haven't liked the look of. Secondhand furniture designed for industrial use—such as metal swivel architects' chairs, library bookcases, and factory pattern-cutting tables—can be incorporated into your home. It can be better quality than its mass-produced equivalents.

tables and chairs

above Stackable contemporary seating with beech-ply frame and splayed metal legs, inspired by the Fifties butterfly chair by Arne Jacobsen.

I like chairs without frills or gimmicky details, in other words, chairs that look good, are robustly constructed, and comfortable. Classic country chairs with rush seats are ideal for kitchens and dining rooms. Fold-up wooden-slatted seats—the staples of church halls the world over—can be stored away and are excellent for use in small spaces. Like chairs, a table should look good, be strong, and a pleasure to sit at. A basic table top perched on trestles—probably one of the most useful and portable shapes—can be set up or collapsed instantly. Secondhand stores are always good sources for chairs and tables alike—take your pick and revamp worn pieces with a coat of paint.

above Big and basic—a definitive kitchen shape in solid pine that can suit all kinds of interiors.

right A crisp bright pink cotton slipcover and a touch of white paint have given a junk chair a new lease on life.

right Perfectly angled to support the sitter's back, this worn but shapely little factory chair is a good example of functional but stylish seating.

below Based on a Fifties shape, a zinc-topped wooden table is a streamlined addition to a gleaming contemporary kitchen.

below You can see examples of this Sixties-style weatherproof aluminium café chair in bars and cafés throughout Europe—a great idea for urban backyards and loft spaces.

below Essential folding shapes for indoors and out: a white slatted chair and a metal dining table.

below Customized with eggshell paint, this simple pine table would make a chic desk or sidetable anywhere in the house.

below A white pickled paint effect is an effective device for sprucing up an old turn-of-the-century pine table like this one.

above A simple trestle table like this one in birchwood-ply has a multitude of uses, ranging from a work desk to an impromtu dining table.

right A fold-up slatted beechwood chair, ideal for storing away in small spaces, and an old wooden straight-back chair—excellent durable seating for kitchens and dining rooms.

below A rustic beech-wood chair with rush seating and a classic beechwood stool.

beds

Beds should be chosen with practical and visual considerations in mind. To guarantee many peaceful nights of slumber, it is crucial at the outset of any bed-buying exercise to invest in a decent mattress and a solid base or frame. If you have limited funds, think about ways of revamping your existing bed. Lovely bedlinen and blankets can disguise even the ugliest studio-bed shapes.

below right A traditional cast iron bed frame suits all kinds of interiors.

below left A Shaker-inspired pine four-poster (an amazingly good value assembly kit) is painted in white eggshell for a smart understated finish.

above Spare in shape and detail and perfectly functional, this superbly streamlined bed in Douglas fir is a minimalist's dream.

above A contemporary shape, excellent for sprawling out on.

right This romantic French daybed is good for tight spaces.

below A Swedish-style wooden sofa with check covers, and a generously proportioned armchair.

sofas and seating

Good springs and sound construction are essential for comfortable upholstered seating. It may be better to buy a good secondhand sofa or armchair with a wooden frame and strong interior springs, stuffing, and webbing than something new and less sturdy. Cover sofas with tough upholstery-weight linen or wool, or devise slipcovers which can be as basic as a throwover sheet or as tailored as a pull-on design in washable.cotton.

this page Laminated drawers with wire baskets are a clever idea for assembly kit kitchen units.

opposite, top right Remember school lockers? This metal mesh closet is great for small spaces.

opposite below, left to right A decorative wooden dresser or visellier like this looks at home in country settings; inexpensively bought from a second-hand store, this simple chest of drawers was improved by a coat of paint; a walk-in closet is one of the most effective ways of stowing away everything from clothes to suitcases.

cupboards and storage

In an ideal world, storage should be designed to allow maximum living and breathing space. In reality we are hampered by budget, cramped rooms, too little time, too many occupants, and too much clutter to set about the task of arranging ourselves a little more efficiently. Here are some ideas to make clearing away a more fruitful and inspiring exercise. Basic wooden shelving is one of the cheapest means of storing everything, from kitchen paraphernalia to bathroom towels, or scores of books. Freestanding storage ideas include simple assembly-kit systems—these are basic structures in pine that are good for utility rooms and children's rooms. If home is an attic room with poor space, build assembly-kit storage systems or closets on site.

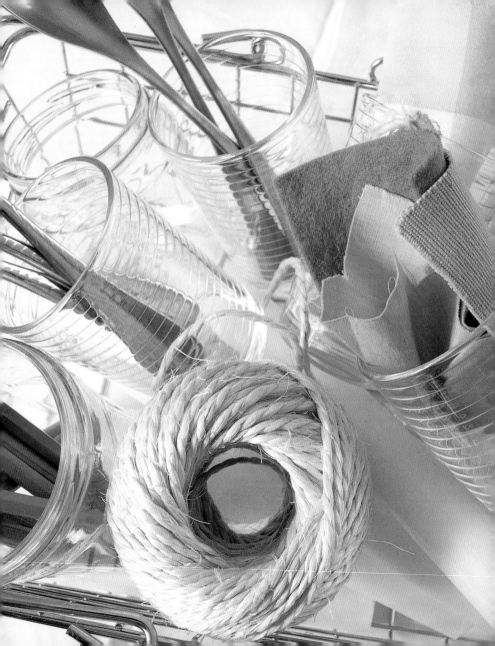

objects

If we each took an inventory of our possessions, how many things would we discover to be useless, or even something that we hated but couldn't give away because it was a present or a family heirloom? It might be painful for your conscience, but in the long run, paring down unnecessary household clutter eases the path to a more practical and soothing existence. Don't be sentimental about hoarding items that you will never use. Identify the things that give you pleasure to hold, to use, and to look at. It is more useful to have one superior saucepan than three second-rate ones that burn everything you cook in them. Even something as basic and utilitarian as a slender wood-and-bristle broom is a thing of beauty and just as humbly aesthetic as the rough mesh structure of a metal strainer or a good old-fashioned mixing bowl whose deep curvy proportions are perfectly evolved to perform its task. Do away with those dusty lamp bases made from Chianti bottles that your mother gave you for your first apartment. But resurrect classic Thirties-style gooseneck desk lamps, as those in the know continue to appreciate them. Vernacular objects perfectly designed to fulfill their function are works of art in their own right.

utensils

A capacious flip-top stainless-steel trashcan will handle large amounts of kitchen garbage, while a wood and bristle broom, found in any hardware store, is an essential tool for sweeping.

Whenever I have to make do with a temporary or makeshift kitchen during house renovations, the surrounding chaos is bearable as long as I have access to water, something to cook on, and a refrigerator. My survival kit of kitchen tools under such siege conditions includes a cast-iron enameled saucepan in which to conjure up everything from breakfast-time oatmeal to herbed chicken casseroles; a sharp knife; a pile of wooden spoons; and, to keep the spirits from flagging and the caffeine levels high, a metal espresso maker that sits on the stove top. Other crucial equipment includes a garlic crusher, scissors, and of course, a decent corkscrew for opening wine.

Some of my favorite tools: a garlic crusher (that also stones olives), a balloon whisk, and lobster crackers, ideal for attacking crab.

What kitchen would be complete without a kettle? Invest in a sturdy and hard-wearing metal catering one for endless rounds of satisfying brew-ups.

A glass citrus fruit juicer is a nifty tool for producing small amounts of orange, lemon, lime, or grapefruit juice.

Produce mounds of crisp, crunchy vegetables that really keep their flavor, or poach small pieces of fish, with a heavy stainless steel steamer.

A robust cast-iron enamelled casserole is excellent, whether you are cooking for a crowd of friends or just for one or two, or preparing a simple family meal.

Drain everything from pasta and rice to salad leaves with a simple metal colander, and borrow or buy a fish kettle to take the angst out of cooking large fish like salmon in one piece.

left Some basic metal tools: a strainer for sifting flour or draining vegetables and a boxy grater for demolishing hunks of cheese such as Parmesan.

left Wonderful to hold, and perfectly proportioned, a stainless-steel frying pan for rustling up everything from risotto to fish steaks.

above Found in most continental kitchens, a classic stove-top espresso maker is an easy way to make steaming-hot strong coffee.

Life would be impossible without a really good sharp stainless-steel knife, a pair of scissors, and a corkscrew!

For seafood treats: a strong oyster knife with a protective guard, and classic cutlery with bone-handled knives.

objects

lighting

We can appreciate that daylight is the perfect light, because there is the dark with which to compare it. But night suffuses everything with its own particular mood and bestows its own impressions and textures. Without darkness we would be deprived of the luxury of candlelight, which is the most sensual, calming, and benign of all sources of light. Lit candles highlight a dark room with a luminous quality that brings us in touch with the sensations of a pre-electric age. For a romantic dining room, invest in a simple chandelier and light it with candles. At its best, artificial lighting is subtle and effective. At its worst, the glaring horrors of rooms with naked light bulbs or the bland brightness of supermarkets and airport waiting rooms speak for themselves. The most sensitive way to light interiors is with pools of subtle illumination, achieved with lamps set in corners or with low-voltage recessed lighting.

above and right For summer evenings, choose from curvy glass hurricane shades, lanterns, and nightlights (easily found in hardware stores).

above right and opposite Utilitarian lamps and work lights look great in contemporary and more traditional settings alike. Overhead pendant lights in spun aluminium work well in kitchen and dining rooms, or as stylish hall lighting. For desk tops, Thirties-style gooseneck lamps are not only smart but flexible practical gadgets that help illuminate all kinds of tasks.

storage

Many small-scale storage ideas can be customized to look individual and imaginative. Reinvent old shoe boxes, for example, by covering them with fabric or paint to provide colorful storage for your home office or for children's toys. Or use a touch of white paint to transform an ugly black clothesrod into a stylish movable closet, ideal for small living spaces. It can be covered with a white sheet to repel dust. I am an avid collector of old jars and other household basics that double as stylish containers, including metal buckets (good for vegetables) and glass mason jars (they make staples like rice, flour, and pasta look good). Industrial meat hooks are available from good kitchen supply stores, and suspended from poles they are a great way to hang up your *batterie de cuisine*.

Empty jam jars with neat, good-looking proportions are ideal for accommodating anything from pens and pencils to flowers.

An ugly black clothes rod has been transformed by a lick of white paint into a stylish and moveable closet, ideal for small living spaces. It can be covered with a white sheet to repel the dust.

left A two-tiered wooden shoe rack, reminiscent of school locker rooms, is useful for halls and bedrooms.

left Display vegetables and other kitchen ingredients in classic aluminum buckets.

right Hang meat hooks from poles for instant hanging space. This old broom handle is supported by metal hardwear.

left Empty wall space can be put to good use with a simple Shaker-style peg rack. These bags are made from a washable cotton.

right Mason storage jars are both utilitarian and stylish and can be filled with staples such as flour, sugar, or pasta.

below Recycle old shoe boxes and cover them with bright cotton fabric as an attractive storage solution in the office, or for children's toys.

left For a smart contemporary look stash spoons and cutlery in metal pots and arrange them in rows on shelves and kitchen surfaces, where they are handy for use.

right A thrift store basket is a useful solution for bulky items such as this thick checked blanket made in Wales and pillows covered in blue and green cotton.

objects

display

Making a statement about the way you display favorite things, from photographs to kitchen pots and pans, is all part of creating an ordered environment and giving your living space a characteristic look. There is something arresting to the eye to see collections of basic vernacular objects—even plain white mugs can look good en masse.

Use natural elements to devise beautifully simple display ideas such as collections of pebbles from the beach; deep shadow boxes filled with leaves, shells, and china fragments from the shoreline; and collections of roughly hewn olive baskets.

left A favorite collection of old bowls is arranged simply in an old corner cupboard.

above Bowls or jars planted with your favorite spring bulbs, and simple, wood-framed shell prints look great arranged in groups.

china and glass

The quality, shape, and size of what you drink out of or eat off is pivotal to relishing what is in your glass or on your plate. I like the ribbed, chunky qualities of Duralex glasses that are robust to drink from. The clean lines and classic proportions of plain white plates also make eating a pleasing affair for both the palate and the eye.

above Creamware china for refreshing brews, including a great big cup for warming milky breakfast coffees.

below Any self-respecting café dispenses strong black espresso coffee in little heavy-bottomed cups with saucers. Imbibing out of anything larger, or flimsier would diminish the experience.

right Blue-and-white spongeware is very decorative for informal settings, and it also looks good in hutches and on shelves.

below Workaday glassware for large drinks of cool iced water and other thirst quenchers.

right Chunky white china mugs from just about any chainstore are essential kitchen items.

Decorative designs for ceramics: blue-and-white tartanware for serving up shortbread, oatcakes and other Scottish treats.

Blue-and-white striped china is bright, basic and comes in lots of versatile shapes. It's great for everyday use.

Jolly blue-and-white checked china is a cheery sight on the breakfast table. This shallow bowl is useful for dishing up cornflakes and other staples.

You can't beat plain blue-and-white bone china for simple and stylish kitchen schemes—one of my all-time favorites.

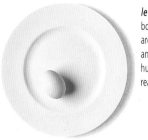

left Classic white bone china plates are my favorites, and make the humblest meal look really appetizing.

Perfectly formed bowl shapes—for serving everything from porridge and puddings to soups and salads.

right This classic jug shape has been around forever and comes in lots of different sizes.

A choice of cups for dedicated coffee drinkers: tiny chocolate brown cups for small shots of pure caffeine, like espresso, or a heavy-bottomed cup for capuccino.

Creamware looks brilliant in country cream painted kitchens, or dining rooms with decorating details in white and other neutrals.

objects

putting it all together

Color and comfort are key ingredients in putting rooms together. Bright, light, airy shades of white and cream, as well as stronger greens, blues, and lavenders create inviting spaces. Choose furniture that combines function with style, and stick to basic shapes. To bring life into your surroundings, think about texture and draw inspiration from nature.

culinary living

An awesome number of items need to be squeezed into the average kitchen: boxes of breakfast cereals, pots, pans, dishwasher, refrigerator, sink—the list is endless. Storing and incorporating them all requires planning and thought. Cupboards, drawers, shelves, and work surfaces should be considered for both functional and aesthetic appeal. Make counters durable and use basic materials like wood, marble, slate, and stainless steel. Pare down your kitchen items to the most basic essentials. Make the daily ritual of eating as pleasurable as is practical. Eat from simple white plates, drink from good glasses, light candles, fill jars with flowers, and spread a crisp white linen cloth for special occasions. Preparing food can be a therapeutic experience even if you are busy with work or family. Avoid food fashions (what is it this month—French, Italian, or outer Mongolian?) and resist long drawn-out recipes with impossible-to-find ingredients. Don't become a nervous wreck looking for exactly the right type of extra-virgin olive oil; if you can't find it, use what you already have. Stick to food that you like and can cook well. It is far better to serve up a simple but excellent cheese on toast than to produce an unremarkable attempt at something more flashy.

Wooden kitchen cupboards and drawers constructed from basic carcasses and painted in tough, matt creamy eggshell textures create understated and smart storage for kitchen items.

In the past, kitchens were purely rooms in which to prepare and cook food, while dining rooms were dedicated to the pleasures of eating. To meet the demands of late 20th-century living, kitchens have evolved as spaces that fulfill many functions, so that eating and living are frequently combined.

Different settings dictate different priorities. Rural kitchens need to cope with the to-ing and fro-ing of muddy feet or paws, and are the natural habitats of wonderful warming stoves such as Vikings, which are practical and stylish machines.

In towns, there is more emphasis on the clever placement of labor-saving devices such as the dishwasher, electric juicer, microwave, and so on, to help deal with the pressures of city life.

right Clean uncluttered kitchens, with pots and pans neatly stored in cupboards or on shelves, are places where you can set a big table and entertain your friends in style.

Most food preparation takes place on durable surfaces and there are various options. Oiled regularly and kept pristine with frequent scrubbing, a counter made of maple or beech is the ultimate luxury, albeit a costly one. A cheaper solution is to buy lengths of beech block from large hardware stores. Salvage yards are also a good source of reclaimed lumber for work surfaces; for example, I found a bargain teak draining board from a Victorian almshouse at a country salvage yard. Despite its association with glossy Hollywood-style bathrooms, marble is a robust, hygienic material, and its unpolished, matte gray, white, or creamy textures make practical, understated work surfaces. Marble is particularly affordable at its source, namely in southern France, Spain, and Italy. For a really cheap kitchen facelift, laminated plywood is available in lengths from lumberyards and comes in many colors. The sink is a crucial part of the kitchen work surface, and deep-white ceramic sinks are ideal and can sometimes be picked up secondhand.

left A bright, cheerful kitchen with a utilitarian feel. Pride of place is given to a magnificent Forties stove that cooks as efficiently as any contemporary model. Blue-and-white checked lino floor tiles and a cotton tablecloth complete the homespun, relaxed atmosphere.

right Open wooden shelving left as bare wood or painted in the same color as the rest of the kitchen is a practical and decorative way to display china, kitchen cans, and containers.

Storage solutions are key to creating a well-organized kitchen. At the most basic level, simple open shelves in pine are incredibly useful for housing plates, glasses, culinary herbs, and just about any other kitchen paraphernalia. Collections of cans and boxes in interesting shapes and colors make an attractive display. Screw cup hooks to the underside of pine shelving and you have instant hanging space for mugs, ladles, strainers, and whisks. Not everyone is eager to have their kitchen contents on view, so cupboard doors hung on a basic frame are the perfect camouflage for canned goods or a repertoire of pots and pans.

Wall-to-wall units and cupboards are practical, but some custom-made schemes with fancy trims and detailing can be fantastically expensive. For a more individual look—and if you are strapped for cash anyway—combine a minimum of built-in elements such as a sink, stove, and counter in a unit, together with free-standing features such as a secondhand hutch jazzed up with paint, or an old metal factory trolley, which is ideal for wheeling plates and dishes around. Other useful storage notions include a wall-mounted wooden plate drainer, or a tall, free-standing cupboard, ideal for filling with heavy items like food cans, groceries, and dishes.

right Blue-and-white striped cotton roller towel, used for chair covers or for table runners as here, can be sourced from specialty companies that supply institutions.

left Crisp plain white cotton tablecloths work in any setting. A row of narcissi planted in large basins creates simple, colorful, and scented decoration for parties and everyday settings alike.

Eating and drinking, however humble and low-key an affair, should be reveled in and made the most of. Deciding what to eat at any particular meal, what to eat it on, and what sort of mood you want to convey are of equal importance. At the end of a grueling day with three children, there are few frills at my table, but it's still worth lighting candles or finding some ironed linen napkins to create a sense of occasion. Table settings need not be elaborate affairs. Pleasing textures and well-made glass, china, and flatware are the crucial elements. On a day-to-day basis, you might settle for a crisp checked cloth with a jar of garden flowers, basic white plates, and simple glass tumblers. When friends come, it is worth making more of an effort and laying a crisp, white linen cloth and napkins, together with candles, your best bone-handled flatware, and wine glasses.

Sales are good sources of discounted china and are where I go to buy seconds of white Wedgwood bone-china plates. Flea markets and thrift stores are useful for finding single pieces of antique glass. During a weekly hunt around my local market in London's East End, I pounced upon half a dozen late-Victorian heavy wine glasses, each one different, and use them to serve up everything from gelatin to drinks.

Department stores, together with an ever-growing number of mail-order companies, are good sources of table linen. Alternatively, you could make your own tablecloths and napkins from special wide linen from fabric wholesalers, or sew fabric by the yard. If you're really stuck, simply use a plain white sheet. And if you have a children's party to organize, buy plain white disposable paper cloths, available from supermarkets.

One of the best things about assembling table settings is thinking of natural greenery and floral components for decoration. In the fall, plates of nuts or leaves look striking as do vases of branches studded with bright red berries. At Christmas time, I spray apples with gold paint and put them in a big wooden bowl for a table decoration or hang them on string from a chandelier. I also scatter small branches of Christmas tree cuttings

Wooden dining chairs come in a variety of shapes. Don't worry if yours aren't all the same design: a mix of styles, sourced from second-hand and junk shops, can look just as good as a fully matching set.

on the table, and for some early seasonal color and scent, I display pots of flowering narcissi or hyacinths. In March and April I like to fill metal buckets with the bright green, sticky buds of chestnut branches or pussy willow, but summer tables are the most fun to create: I pick nasturtiums and sweet peas from my backyard and bring home armfuls of Queen Anne's lace after a day out in the countryside. Even a few jars of fresh herbs—thyme, rosemary, lavender, or parsley—make basic but beautiful decorations. Sometimes we've rented a cottage in the country, and there the summer hedges are thick with leggy purple foxgloves that make stunning table embellishments simply stuffed into tall, clear glass vases.On trips to Spain, everyone eats outside in the evening, sitting around trestle tables laid with grilled fish, meat, pasta, bread, wine, and cheese. After the glut of wild spring blooms such as orchids, daisies, buttercups, campion, and lilies, it's harder to find flowers during the months of summer drought. A useful source is the local farmer's market where Spanish ladies sell white tuberoses, a few stems of which produce a glorious, intoxicating scent as night falls. Otherwise, the table is decorated with vases of silvery gray olive cuttings. We get the barbeque going and cook up everything from sardines to slivers of bell pepper.

opposite page Plain white china plates, bowls, and cups look great against any color scheme, and always make food look appealing, however humble it may be. Specialty catering stores can often yield good buys.

this page Soft lilac paint on the walls is a good foil for covers in muslin and a plain white cloth. A lime green checked cotton curtain and single stems of purple anemones provide a colorful contrast in this fresh and inviting dining set-up for two.

Table embellishments can be simple yet striking:

left Topiary shapes work well in terra-cotta flower pots. Try a leggy myrtle standard, like the one shown here, or other shapes in box or bay.

right A pretty candelabra, a lucky find in a Roman market, looks especially lovely at night.

The seating arrangement of any dining area depends upon space. If it is limited, tables and chairs might need to be of the fold-up variety and stored away if necessary. On the other hand, generously proportioned rooms can accommodate big wooden refectory tables, or oval and round shapes, and deep comfortable seating. Do not worry about having sets of matching chairs; disparate shapes, especially secondhand wooden kitchen chairs, can look quite good together, and if you want to create a sense of unity, you can cover them in simple pull-on slipcovers in muslin, woven cotton, or some other durable and washable texture. (See page 75 for some colorful examples in blue-and-white striped roller-towel cotton.)

culinary living

right Low-backed wooden office chairs on wheels, and a mahogany door on metal trestles are inventive ideas that are well suited to the contemporary living space in this converted London industrial building.

Choose a table to suit the style of the rest of the dining area. Rustic farmhouse shapes in wood look good almost anywhere and are practical and robust. Very contemporary streamlined models with zinc, stainless-steel, or laminated surfaces suit more modern settings.

right and below Refectory style: a plain table and benches in solid Douglas fir pine are spare and minimal solutions for dining. Equally streamlined are the full-length limestone bench seating down one wall and the open fireplace.

If furniture classics are your penchant, look to early 20th-century designs, such as the simple ladderback oak chairs and solid oak tables, or more recent classics such as the sensually molded, white bucket-shaped, Tulip chairs from the Fifties (see page 81). Since most people prefer brand new dining sets, excursions to flea markets and probing through secondhand stores can yield fantastic buys at bargain prices. If you need to create extra table space for a party, you can make a very basic dining table from a piece of board or even an old door laid over a pair of trestles. Simply disguise the makeshift base under a plain white sheet.

Other useful elements for dining areas include a side table or sideboard from which to serve food or to display flowers or lighting. It's always handy to have a supply of plates, bowls, and glasses close at hand, either stored on open shelving or in cabinets.

One of the highlights of winter is enjoying an open fire. If you are lucky enough to have a working fireplace, gather some logs and kindling (or be practical and have them delivered!) and give your guests the luxury of a warming blaze. Candlelight is the best and most romantic light to eat by. I buy cream-colored church candles from a candlemaker at a nearby Greek Orthodox Church. If you don't possess particularly nice candlesticks, set the candles on plain white plates, or leave them free-standing for subtle illumination.

far right Colorful treatments for dining rooms include the yellow, green, and blue scheme shown here. Pale cream walls in eggshell paint create a plain backdrop for splashes of more vibrant colors such as blue-and-white checked cotton Roman blinds, sofa cushions in lime green and blue, and a simple metal chandelier in matt yellow. On the table, the plastic green checked cloth, available by the yard from department stores, is smart and practical for everyday use. Flowering spring bulbs, bought cheaply by the tray from a local market, and planted in painted flowerpots, provide scent and sunny detail.

relaxed living

Even the most frenetic workaholics need time to sink into comfortable chairs, put their feet up, and contemplate life. It's good to be nurtured by music, soft throw pillows, or a blazing fire. Living rooms are tailored to meet the demands of their occupants— families with small children require battleproof chairs and fabrics, while single individuals with no danger of sabotage by sticky hands might make a sumptuous wall-to-wall white scheme their priority. But whatever your family status, gender, or age, comfort and texture are the most important factors for the rooms in which you want to wind down. Use colors that soothe, and are light-enhancing—such as soft creams or bone whites—and keep paint textures matte. Buy solid, comfortable upholstery and proper, feather-filled throw pillows. Be selective with the fabric textures that you use. Seek out tough linens in beautiful creams and naturals or strong woven cottons in ticking, checked, and striped designs. Experiment with bright plain colors such as blue, green, pink, and orange. Explore the variety of warm woolen fibers, for use as upholstery covers, soft throws, or insulating drapes. Be imaginative and buy yards of cheap gauze to make delicate drapes.

A living room should be a comfortable and relaxed area where you can sprawl out on a sofa with a good book, listen to music, watch television, or simply sit back and think. Color, comfort, texture, and warmth are important for putting together an agreeable, functional space.

From draperies to slipcovers, fabric colors can change a room as much as the impact of paint.

far right French metal daybeds can be found in salesrooms and antique shops and look great with striped cotton ticking bolsters or plain white cushions or throws. Paint them white or leave them bare.

right Blue-and-white is fresh with decorative details like crisp striped throw pillows and scrunchy Roman shades, faded floral covers, and lots of checked cotton accessories.

Don't worry about slavishly matching the throw pillow to the curtain lining or the ties on your favorite slipcover. It is much more interesting to try similar but contrasting fabric shades. I remember a room I decorated in a spring theme where cream-yellow walls contrasted with bright green-and-white checked blinds, together with slipcovers in a dark cabbage-leaf color and throw pillows in a lime-green and blue-and-white thinly-striped cotton. The effect was bright, sunny, and very easy to live with.

Living rooms must be comfortable, and comfort relies partly on well-made and sturdy upholstery. It is more satisfactory to invest in a good-quality secondhand couch, say, than something that is brand new, mass-produced, and lightweight.

I know an enterprising woman who sells everything from hand-me-down Knole sofas taken from mansions to junk armchairs, all to be found piled up in sheds at her farmhouse. If you invest in new upholstery, test it for comfort before buying: sit on it for ten minutes, bounce up and down on the seat (you should be able to feel the underlying support); lean back (you should not feel any springs protruding from the framework); lift it to test the weight of the framework (it should not be too lightweight).

Upholstery fabric should be hardwearing. Some of the best fabrics are linen and linen-cotton mixes. A few years ago I found some wonderful earth-colored linen at a fabric outlet, on sale at fifteen percent off. I bought up ten yards which was enough to cover a Victorian chesterfield. Despite heavy wear and tear from parties, children, dogs, and cats, it still looks respectable, only of course I am now itching to find another bargain. Slipcovers are a practical way of cleaning and an economical way of updating sofas and chairs, and can be made with various details such as pleated or simple box

Blues, greens, and grays are useful color tools.

right Powder blue paintwork looks sharp against bold navy striped slipcovers and pillows in assorted shades of blue cotton stripe. White brickwork walls and whitened parquet flooring emphasize the airy feel.

far left A painted gray skirting adds subtle definition to plain white walls in a light and fresh Provençal sitting room. Reclaimed terra-cotta tiles laid in an uneven pattern add to the vernacular effect.

above Warming not cold: rich blue-green emulsion paint makes a distinctive foil for white woodwork, a plain white dustsheet throw and polished wooden floorboards.

this page Splashes of terra-cotta act as glowing detail in the cream-colored living room of a London Georgian townhouse. Among furnishing and fabrics in blues, greens, and yellows there is a kelim rug in faded earth and brick. Spread across the marble mantlepiece are old clay pots and a rosemary wreath. Other rich ingredients seen below include old wooden Spanish soup bowls filled with rag balls made of scraps of checked and striped cotton and an antique three-legged milking stool.

far right A fold-up butler's tray acts as a versatile display idea with a candlestick lamp, and a jug of spring flowers.

skirts, matching ties at the corners, or a row of buttons or a bow at the back. If you want an instant update, cover an unattractive sofa with a white sheet or a simple gingham-checked cotton throw. This is also a good idea for giving upholstery a change for the summer.

You can create a wonderful room with a great color scheme and lots of decorative ideas, but if it's cold, it's miserable. The ultimate in warmth and atmosphere is a blazing log fire—and woods such as chestnut and apple give off delicious smokey scents. Smokeless coal is an ecological second-best fuel. Not everyone has access to wood or the inclination to lay and maintain a real fire, so flame-effect fires are worth considering. Although they don't throw out as much heat as a real fire and can look artificial, they are not a bad compromise and many of the modern versions do a great job of fooling you into thinking they are real. Underfloor heating schemes involve hidden pipes connected to the central-heating system and are a great way of dispensing with unsightly radiators.

this page Neutral tones of white and cream create a peaceful feeling with simple picture frames and streamlined lighting.

right Contemporary details include market finds such as a Sixties basket chair, and sunburst mirror.

far right Harking back to Fifties gum commercials, the owner of this cozy paneled living room in a traditional shingled house on Long Island aptly describes the subtly colored paintwork as chewing-gum gray. Rough sisal matting, pine planking (resourcefully salvaged from packing crates), and neutral-colored linen add to the fresh and understated effect.

Pillows are important comfort factors. Buy proper feather or kapok-filled pads; foam fillings are unsightly and lumpy. Pillow forms squeezed into stingy covers don't look good, so make covers roomy and allow the pillow to "breathe." Simple piped throw pillows or flanged shapes are perennial classics. Bags with tie openings look good and are incredibly easy to sew at home. You can make pillows out of just about any fabric—I like tough blue-and-white checked Indian cotton, striped ticking, and light cotton in bright shades (which is good for a summery feel). You can also sew new covers by using material from old curtains, table cloths, scraps of fabric in your favorite colors or patterns. Anything faded and floral, especially blues and whites or soft pinks and lavenders will work well with checks, stripes, and solids. If, say, you hanker after a beautiful floral cotton but can't afford the hefty price tag for a big soft furnishing project, why not buy just half a yard—the same cost as the average price of a pair of shoes, and make it up into a beautiful throw pillow for a favorite chair. It will last considerably longer than the shoes!

right For a homespun feel with an updated edge, this loft space has been decorated with pristine white walls, galvanized metal buckets and a primitive-style metal chandelier. Woven checked cotton bought in a sale has been used to make simple slipcovers for a battered old couch and chairs.

above More homespun ideas: disparate furniture from a sale is unified with soft gray paint.

Deep-pile, wall-to-wall white carpet might be appropriate in a boudoir-like bedroom, but for stylish, everyday living, natural flooring textures such as coir, sisal, seagrass, and cotton or wool rugs in checks and stripes are more liveable with in terms of cost and practicality. For insulation, lay rugs over one another. Buy mats that are bound with burlap or woven cotton borders as they look better and don't fray. Cotton rugs are cheap, and many are designed to be thrown in the washing machine, but remember that very bright colors might run, so they should be carefully hand-washed. Thick tartan-plaid wool rugs are a good investment.

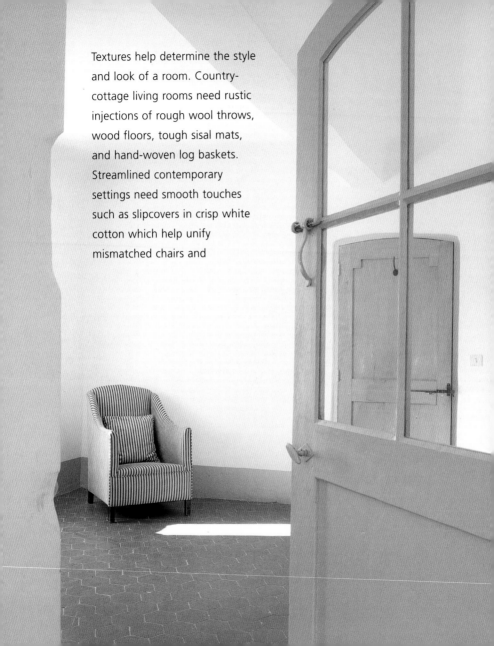

Textures help determine the style and look of a room. Country-cottage living rooms need rustic injections of rough wool throws, wood floors, tough sisal mats, and hand-woven log baskets. Streamlined contemporary settings need smooth touches such as slipcovers in crisp white cotton which help unify mismatched chairs and

below and opposite
Comfortable yet functional living spaces with seating covered in robust ticking or muslin.

left A small space set aside for a home study area successfully houses vital office elements, including a basic trestle table, a metal filing cabinet, cardboard box files revamped with paint, and a smart metal Twenties-style desk lamp.

complement pale wood floors. Modern materials such as zinc and aluminum for lighting and table surfaces also emphasize a more up-to-date look.

Curtains and drapes take substantial amounts of fabric, but need not break the bank. Stick to simple headings such as loops and ties. Choose strong cottons and linens. If you buy ten yards or more from fabric wholesalers, many will

relaxed living

Simple shapes in plain fabrics create light and airy window treatments:

below Light cotton curtains draped to the floor. They are simply tied onto a metal pole, bought by the length and bent over at the ends.

left Heavy canvas with eyelets can be hooked onto a window frame and pulled back as required.

right Fresh and filmy: soft cream-colored linen curtains with a decorative double-layered heading, recycled by the owner from a previous apartment. The wooden pole and rings are painted to create a unifying effect.

give you a substantial discount. Line curtains for a better "hang" and also to protect them against fading due to sunlight. Interlinings give greater insulation; bump is the thickest and looks like a blanket, while domette is a brushed cotton and the most commonly used. Roman or plain windowshades are useful for providing extra insulation with curtains, as well as protecting from the sun. Shades also suit just about any window shape. I like Roman shades and I have examples in checked cotton and plain muslin hanging at my Georgian windows; these are all hand washable in the bath. Unlined curtains in filmy textures such as voile and organdy are cheap, stylish options. If you live in a climate with hot summers and cold winters, have two sets of curtains, light ones for the summer and warmer pairs of thermal ones for the winter. Paint curtain poles the same color as walls for a unifying effect. Inexpensive ideas for poles include wooden doweling from lumberyards cut to length and painted, and stretchy wire available from hardware stores that is ideal for small drops, for example, in cottage windows.

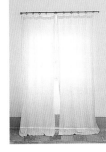

sleeping in style

We do so much of it that sleep deserves to be
a peaceful and luxuriating experience. On a cold
winter's night, it is bliss to curl up in crisp white
bedlinen and warm wooly blankets. Conversely, in
summer it's good to lie with the sparest of
bedclothes, say just a fine cotton sheet and an open
window to catch a cooling nighttime breeze.
Bedrooms need to be quiet airy refuges away from
domestic distractions. There should be lots of
cupboards, boxes, or ample closet space to store
clothing and clutter. Some of the best ideas include
spacious built-in, walk-in closets with simple paneled
doors. Old laundry baskets, big wooden boxes, and
even old shoe boxes covered in fabric and paint are
also useful bedroom storage notions. Bedroom
textures need to be soft and inviting, such as gauze
curtains, plain muslin blinds, fine cotton pajamas,
and fluffy toweling robes. Soft wool checked
blankets in cream or blue are great for dressing beds.
Then there are antique quilts, with pretty floral
designs, that look lovely folded or draped over a
bedstead. Spend as much as you can afford on
bedding—soft goosedown duvets and pillows are the
ultimate bedtime luxury. It is also prudent to invest in
a strong mattress that does not sag and bend.

Comfort factors in bedrooms include freshly laundered sheets and warm cream-colored wool blankets. Search markets and second-hand store for old bedlinen; the quality is often better than modern textures. Worth looking out for are old damask bed covers and fine embroidered linen pillow cases. Sleep peacefully in a traditional bedstead: classic brass always looks wonderful, and decorative ironwork looks great painted white. Create an calm of oasis with a clutter-free room.

A bedroom is a sanctuary, away from work and other people. It is a place where you can curl up between crisp sheets with a good book to read, a hot drink, and a bar of chocolate. Asleep or not, all of us spend so much time there that it should be the one room in the house where we can be indulgent. Bedroom textures should be luxurious, soft, and warm. The stresses of the day fall away when you climb into white cotton sheets, curl up under soft blankets, and warm yourself up in cold weather. It pays to invest in the best bedding you can afford and to take time in choosing the right bed.

There are all sorts of bed shapes to suit the look you want to achieve. At a basic level, there is a studio bed which can be dressed quite simply. It is useful in a bedroom that doubles as a daytime living room or study.

I prefer bright and airy bedrooms in whites and creams—rooms that have a light ambience throughout the year. Darker, richer colors may suit some individuals, but waking up to moody walls on dark mornings during a long winter may quickly become a gloomy prospect. Bedrooms need to be comfortable, optimistic places, with supplies of good reading matter, soft bedside lighting, some sort of seating, and maybe a bowl of favorite flowers.

There is nothing to beat the simplicity of plain white bedlinen. It is smart, stylish, and unassuming. When an injection of color is desired, you can look to bold, contemporary designs, perhaps in tomato red, lime green, fuchsia pink, or lemon yellow. Bedlinens in such colors work particularly well in southern climates with strong light. It seems that country style with its fussy floral-patterned sheets and pillowcases has had its day on the decoration scene (and none too soon). But for the mass market, manufacturers persist in launching frilly, flowery designs that make beds look like the tops of

chocolate boxes. However, florals in the bedroom can look really pretty if used carefully and with restraint. Take for example, a simple lavender-colored country bedroom theme, suitable for a cottage bedroom. You can make basic pillowcases in a delicate rosebud print and combine them with white sheets and pillowcases, and a faded antique floral patchwork quilt. Stick to a plain cotton window treatment, paint the walls white, and cover the floors in cheap, neutral cotton rugs.

left Gray paintwork and a simple painted bedside table, together with a subtlely checked blue wool blanket and a glass of vibrant yellow spring daffodils, inject color to the overall neutral effect created by the white walls and bedlinen in this restful Provençal farmhouse bedroom.

this page Brilliant blues lend a seaside air to a Long Island bedroom. Blue-and-white patchwork quilts, boldly striped cotton pillowcases, and white painted walls add to the bright and breezy feel.

right A romantic mahogany *bateau lit* is a great vehicle for layer upon layer of wonderful white antique bedlinen. A filmy mosquito net, functional as well as decorative, is generously swathed from the ceiling to complete the translucent effect.

this page Distinctive in texture and color, smooth polished parquet flooring and bentwood furniture are smart, dark contrasts to creamy walls and bedlinen in a Parisian apartment.

Forced to make up my own bed from an early age, I think that an orderly, uncluttered bedroom helps to set you up mentally for whatever difficulties and chaos you may come across during the day. Storage, of course, is a key issue. It is quite surprising how a few pieces of casually flung clothing or perhaps a modest pile of discarded newspapers create a bedroom scene that begins to look like a rummage sale. Built-in shelves with doors along one wall are a very successful way of storing clothes, hats, shoes, bags, suitcases, and other closet necessities. Free-standing armoires and chests are useful, but impractical if space is tight. If you are restricted to a budget, you can always curtain an alcove with muslin, linen, or even an old bedspread. Except for a couple of hours spent at the sewing machine, the results are almost instantaneous and very stylish.

A large chest of drawers is always useful for swallowing up smaller items of clothing and spare bedlinen. Old trunks, big boxy laundry baskets, and modern-looking zinc boxes are also useful bedroom storage devices.

Bedsteads offer a variety of decorative possibilities. A Shaker-style painted wooden four-poster frame looks good with tie-on curtains, a muslin or linen valance, or left entirely bare. Good-value examples are available in assembly kit form, nineteenth-century French metal daybeds are

left A country feel is evoked by matte painted paneling, a green wooden bed, and simple fabrics and furnishings in a Georgian townhouse. An antique lavender-colored patchwork quilt with a seaweed design and pink sprigged floral pillowcases, run up in lawn dress fabric, provide colorful and fresh detail.

excellent for dual-purpose rooms and look really smart with ticking bolsters and pillows; they are not difficult to find if you track down dealers who specialize in antique French decorative furniture. If there are children in the family, consider bunk beds. Available in most department stores or large furniture warehouses, they are a very good value and can be dressed up with a coat of paint.

Those of us who enjoy the pleasures of a firm bed know that high-quality bedding really does help toward getting a good night's sleep. The best type of mattress is sewn to size with layers of white curled hair, together with

sleeping in style

111

this page Hot shots: vivid splashes of bright color work well in sunny, southern climates. Experiment with cool cotton bedlinen in bold blue, green, yellow, pink, and orange. As temperatures soar, practical ideas for keeping cool are essential: windows flung wide let air flow through, light muslin curtains help to catch a breeze, and stone floor tiles stay cool underfoot.

far right Bunk beds are an economical and useful idea for children's bedrooms—they are space-saving as well as being fun to sleep in. Update and give a stylish look to plain pine bunks with pale eggshell paint as seen here.

fleece wool and white cotton felt, all incorporated with solid box springs. Perfect pillows are combinations of duck down and feather, gray duck feather, or the ultimate luxury, white goose feather. It is worth your while spending a little bit more when it comes to buying bedding, both for increased comfort and longevity.

My dream is to sleep in linen sheets that are laundered and pressed daily. Until this fantasy is realized, I shall be content with a box of assorted cotton linens at various stages of wear and tear. My softest sheets are Egyptian cotton, bought years ago and still going strong. I also love antique bedlinen and have various Victorian linen and cotton lace pillow-cases, as well as the odd linen sheet handed down from elderly relatives or bought in thrift stores and flea markets. Although pure linen sheets are very costly and need extra care and maintenance, they will last a lifetime. Secondhand linen should be clean and starched, and feel crisp and tightly woven. Modern linens shed creases faster than traditional ones, reducing the need for ironing.

Duvets have become an almost universal item of bedding, but sheets and blankets are still popular. The practical thing about layers of bedclothes is that you can simply peel back or pull on the layers to suit the temperature. In spring, for example, a cotton blanket and sheet may be all that is necessary and, when the air conditioning is on in midsummer, nothing beats the addition of a wool blanket.

clean living

To start the day, an invigorating shower, or simply a wash in a basin of hot water, wakes you up and triggers circulation. At other times, and especially at the end of the day, I can spend hours soaking in a tub of steaming hot water, listening to the radio (sneaking off for a mid-afternoon session is also highly recommended for a rare treat). They may not be the best at conserving heat, but smooth cast-iron baths are definitely the most agreeable to soak in. It's good to scent the water with fragrant oil or work up a creamy lather with soap. A bleached wooden bathrack is a useful vehicle for storing soaps and washcloths and keeping reading material dry and within reach. Loofahs, sponges, and brushes are also essential bathroom tools for keeping skin pristine and well scrubbed. To accompany daily washing rituals, use fluffy cotton towels in white, seaside blues, and bright spring-green colors. Bathrobes in toweling or soft waffle cotton are also delicious ways of drying off—buy big sizes for really wrapping up well. The best showers soak you with a powerful delivery of water, and have finely tuned faucets that deliver hot or cold water as you require it. Invest in duckboards and soft cotton bathmats to mop up the inevitable pools of water.

clean living

A bath, a shower, or even a quick face splash are instant revivers and help relieve the stresses of daily living. Like eating, washing can be a deliciously sensual ritual. It can vary from a short, sharp, invigorating cold outdoor shower on a hot summer's day to a more languid experience in midwinter when a long, hot, steaming bath is the perfect antidote to dark days and icy temperatures. Copious supplies of hot water are at the top of my list of crucial bathroom ingredients—even the meanest, drab, and cramped little bathroom can be acceptable if it delivers piping-hot water, and plenty of it. Scented soaps and lotions are essential elements too. Among my favorites are delicately scented rosewater soap and rose geranium bath gel. If I'm in the mood for more pungent aromas, I choose stronger scented spicy soaps with warming tones.

White bathrooms are bright, light, and airy, as shown by the gleaming examples pictured here. Walls and woodwork are in varying shades of white together with pristine clean ceramic tiles, baths and sinks. Deliciously tactile textures include big fluffy towels, soft sponges, and tough cottons for laundry bags.

right Real Forties bathrooms were cold clammy places with peeling linoleum floors and intermittent hot water issued from unpredictable boilers. The sea-green and white Long Island bathroom here might be retro in feeling, but is very modern in its comforting supplies of heat and hot water. Simple and functional, it houses a sturdy cast-iron bath on ball-and-claw feet, a plain wooden mirrored bath cabinet, and a painted stool for resting a bathtime drink. Seek out ideas for recreating this relaxed, utilitarian look by rummaging around in second-hand stores for big white clinical enamel jugs (the sort that hospitals used for washing babies), old formica-topped tables, metal buckets and medicine cabinets, or old versions of the wooden bathmat above.

Luxurious yet eminently achievable bathroom ideas include a glass candelabra for bathing by candlelight, and a comfortable chair with soft toweling seating. Practical bathroom storage ideas include woven cane laundry baskets and junk objects like old metal school shoe lockers or tin boxes used to house soaps, lotions, and other paraphernalia.

Indispensable for drying big white cotton bath sheets and white rag-rug Portuguese bathmats is my Thirties-style heated chrome towelrod. To finish off my ablutions, I love to wrap up in a soft, white seersucker bathrobe—they're rather expensive, but well worth it for a daily dose of luxury.

Choosing a bathtub is a matter of taste as well as practical consideration. Traditional-style, free-standing cast-iron bathtubs with ball-and-claw feet are deep and look good, but they need sturdy floors to support their weight, the considerable weight of a tubful of water, plus the weight of the bather. In contrast, modern acrylic baths are light, warm to the touch, and come in lots of shapes.

Enameled steel baths are strong and hardwearing but, like modern acrylic baths, they need the support of a frame. For stylish details, either box the bathtub with plain white tiles, or make a border of tongue-and-groove wood panels, which can be painted or waxed for protection.

Bathroom textures and surfaces need to be hardwearing and easy to maintain. Wipe bathtubs, washbasins, and showers daily with soapy water while they are still warm.

Old ceramic jugs, weathered wooden shelves with cut-out patterns, cheap painted peg rails, and seashell prints are key elements for a traditional feel.

Get the look and create your own Georgian-inspired bathroom with sludgy matte eggshell paint, an old-fashioned bathtub on a raised platform, and big weathered brass faucets. Hide elements of contemporary life behind plain paneled closets. Seal wooden floors in matte varnish or use thick cotton bathmats to soak up water from dripping bodies.

above Daily ablutions are an uplifting experience in this bright and cheery sea green and blue theme. Solid functional fittings that were happily left intact for the owner included a splendid old ceramic sink on a stand with classic faucets and visible fittings.

Try not to use abrasive cleaners, which can cause damage to many surfaces and glazes; choose softer sponges or cloths instead.

Ceramic sinks, lavatories, toilets, and shower stalls are widely available and offer a good value. Ceramic tiles for floors and walls provide a good splashproof environment. Well-sealed wooden floors are acceptable, as are terra-cotta or linoleum floors, provided they are properly laid to stop water

The average bathroom store has a pretty paltry selection of taps and unremarkable shapes can be costly. Here are some inspiring ideas.

far left A single stainless steel spout with an artfully concealed faucet mechanism.

above Brass taps from a builder's yard.

left Chunky Victorian pillar faucets found in a London salvage yard.

clean living

opposite Introduce color to bathrooms with bright towels and marine-blue and lime-green robes.

right Swimming-pool inspired tiny blue mosaic tiles are an inventive idea for a walk-in shower space. Equally resourceful are basic stainless-steel kitchen mixer faucets reinvented as a shower spout.

from seeping underneath and causing damage. Avoid carpet—sooner or later it will get wet and will rapidly become moldy and smelly.

When planning a shower, check that you have enough water pressure to produce a powerful downpour. You might need a pump that boosts the flow. Showers can be simple affairs—from a hand set mounted on the bathtub faucet with a protective screen or curtain, to a state-of-the-art walk-in room with a shower that delivers a deluge of water.

There are numerous ways of storing bathroom equipment. Built-in cabinets are useful and should, if possible, be big enough for keeping towels and other bathlinens on hand. Boxes and baskets are good for storing dirty linen, spare towels, toilet brushes, sponges, and other cleaning supplies.

outdoor living

When the temperature rises and the days lengthen, images of summer reappear—like dirt between the toes, warm bare skin, icy drinks, and creased cool linen—and it's time to head outside. Dedicated outdoor lovers will already have grabbed the pleasures of those first few tentative days of spring when it's a revelation to see and feel the sun again after months of dreary winter. They pack picnic baskets and blankets and take the first excursion of the season. Given a sunny day and appropriate clothing, I will pack a thermos of hot soup and smoked salmon and cream-cheese bagels and head off with my family to an empty stretch of south coast beach for a picnic.

Then, once summer is well established, there is that feeling that it will go on forever and everyone becomes complacent and irritated with the heat, humidity, and mosquitoes. But when the days are long and the evenings balmy, what a luxury it is to eat breakfast, lunch, and supper al fresco. Invigorating as well as relaxing, the event can be as simple as drinking coffee at a sidewalk café— something blissful for city dwellers—or a weekend picnic in the park with the best cheese, bread, and wine that you can afford.

Eating outside is one of life's sensual pleasures. Whatever the scenario, from a windswept beach beneath racing clouds to a warm, flower-scented night, the taste and texture of food seems enhanced when eaten out in the elements. The British, for instance, have always been fond of picnics, packing thermoses, blankets, raincoats, and quantities of ham sandwiches to face unpredictable weather with determination. In complete contrast, Spaniards give in to fiercely hot summer afternoons

left Keep cool with a shady awning made from sheets of cane spread over a simple iron framework. Other ideas for retreating out of the sun include panels of canvas stretched hammock-style across a small courtyard, patio or between trees. For a more permanent arrangement that can be stored over the winter months, invest in a big canvas umbrella on metal or wooden frames. I've seen good ones in basic green-and-white stripes, designed for use on the beach but equally at home in the back yard or country.

right The only rule for food served outside is that is should be delicious and easy to eat.

and laze around shady tables idling over jamón, bread, wine, and steaming paellas cooked on camping stoves.

The passion for eating al fresco has grown with me into adult life. Childhood picnics are remembered for their delicious informality, where for once adults did not bother with knives and forks or insist on elbows being off the table, or even mind if you sprawled out, sandwich in hand. Inspired by books such as Elizabeth David's *Summer Cooking*, my picnics might include French bread soaked with olive oil and garlic, and stuffed with goat's cheese and anchovies. Everything is stored in a plain, but eminently practical ice chest, together with drinks of beer, bubbly

wine, or crisp dry Manzanilla sherry.

At home, my tiny backyard becomes an extra room in summer. There is not much sun, but climbing roses and clematis manage to thrive, and flowerpots filled with herbs add color, texture, and culinary detail. As soon as the temperature allows, we set up green metal folding chairs around a big wooden table. I spread the table with white or blue-and-white checked cloths together with jars of roses, nasturtiums, or Queen Anne's lace. In the evening, candles set in flowerpots provide a wonderful glow and do not blow out with every gust of wind. Sometimes we eat fresh barbecued salmon steaks, sardines, or mackerel

outdoor living

stuffed with parsley, lemon, and garlic. For dessert I make strawberry or raspberry ice cream with the help of a small electric ice cream machine and serve it with summer berries and shortcake.

Equipment for eating out in the open has never been so varied. Camping goods outlets are good sources for coolers, stoves, and traditional enamel tin plates and mugs. Sleek, streamlined, shatterproof vacuum flasks are useful for keeping fluids as hot or as cold as you want. Outdoor furniture ideas include fold-up slatted chairs that can be stored away easily in winter. If your budget does not run to an expensive patio table, then cheat with an old door laid across trestles, covered with a cloth in a favorite fabric.

Durable, portable, and attractive outdoor ideas: folding wooden tables and chairs (these were borrowed from the local village bar in Spain but similar ones can be found in second-hand furniture stores); lengths of cotton for tablecloths, pillows for comfort; bright yellow plastic tumblers; woven olive baskets; and jars packed with freshly picked herbs for decoration.

credits

page 1 checked cotton Ikea; jug Heal's; tea towels Crate & Barrel, USA

page 2 room painted in Nantucket Benjamin Moore USA

page 4 Provençal chairs Paris junk shop

page 6 cotton drill Z. Butt Textiles

page 7 interior design Susie Manby

page 10 enamel jugs Ruby Beets Antiques, USA

page 11 ribbed glass The Conran Shop; candles Price's Candles

page 14 tea towels Wolfman Gold & Good Co., USA; chair cover fabric Laura Ashley; plates and jugs from a selection at Pottery Barn, USA; bowl Habitat

page 15 paint swatches from top: Sanderson Spectrum 22-1 Lavender White, Sanderson Spectrum 7-13 Marble White; Sanderson Spectrum 4-10 Winter White, Dulux 0005-Y Tremble, Dulux 0705-Y Sunbleached, Sanderson Spectrum 04-09 Neutral

Page 16 paint swatches from top: John Oliver Winter Sky, Dulux 1520-B10G Relaxation, Sanderson Spectrum 26-04 Lupine Blue, Dulux 1030-R80B Bridesmaid, Sanderson

Spectrum 24-11 Wood Hyacinth; plastic beaker Heal's

page 17 striped table mat Crate & Barrel; junk chair painted in Sanderson Spectrum 24-04 Swiss blue eggshell; plate Anta; checked tray John Lewis

page 18 paint swatches from top: Sanderson Spectrum 41-03 Springtime, Sanderson Spectrum 40-04 Sunny Green, Sanderson Spectrum 39-03 Salad Green, Dulux 1520-G Lily Root, Farrow & Ball 23 Powder Blue, Farrow & Ball 32 Cooking Apple Green

page 19 coffee cup and saucer Designers Guild

page 20 paint swatches from bottom: Sanderson Spectrum 23-09 Fascination, Sanderson Spectrum 21-10 Fidelity, Sanderson Spectrum 21-17 Lavender Lave, Sanderson Spectrum 21-04 Lilac, Dulux 1040-R70B Harlequin; lavender paper and folder from a selection at Paperchase; plastic brush Designers Guild

page 21 Bunny chair Designers Guild; pillow fabric Manuel Canovas

page 22 napkins Habitat

page 23 paint swatches from bottom: Dulux 2030-Y70R Campfire, Farrow & Ball 39 Fowler Pink, Farrow & Ball 45 Sand, Dulux 3050-Y50R Free Range, Sanderson

Spectrum 50–23 Salisbury; pots Clifton Nurseries

page 24 chair cover fabric Habitat; wall painted in Country Cream, Dulux

page 25 paint swatches from top: Dulux 0030-Y10R Jigsaw, Dulux 1030-Y Spring Butter, Farrow & Ball 44 Cream, Sanderson Spectrum 6-23 Gobi Tan, Farrow & Ball 15 Bone; throw Colefax & Fowler

pages 26–27 plate Ruby Beets Antiques, USA

page 28 galvanized metal storage box Ikea; wooden and metal cutlery from a selection at Wolfman Gold & Good Co., USA

page 30 sisal mat John Lewis

pages 36–37 fabrics from top: cotton stripe; cotton check; cotton check; cotton check (all by Designers Guild); plain green cotton The Conran Shop; cotton roller towel by Universal Towel Company; cotton by The Conran Shop; cotton mix stripe by John Lewis; cotton ticking by Russell & Chapple; cotton check by Ikea; cotton ticking by Ian Mankin; cotton stripe by Laura Ashley

pages 38–39 1 cotton sheeting John Lewis 2 cotton voile Wolfin Textiles 3 cotton Muriel Short 4 polyester/cotton muslin Laura Ashley 5 cotton muslin Wolfin Textiles 6 cotton stripe The Conran Shop 7 cotton check The Conran Shop 8 cotton check The Conran Shop 9 self-checked cotton voile Habitat 10 silk Pongees 11 cotton voile check Habitat 12 cotton voile Laura Ashley 13 printed cotton tana lawn Liberty 14 cotton chambray McCulloch & Wallis 15 cotton calico Wolfin Textiles16 cotton Wolfin Textiles 17 cotton muslin Muriel Short 18 cotton stripe Ian Mankin 19 cotton Habitat 20 cotton Designers Guild 21 polyester/cotton muslin Laura Ashley 22 linen Wolfin Textiles 23 natural linen Wolfin Textiles 24 cotton muslin Muriel Short 25 cotton muslin Muriel Short 26 cotton The Conran Shop 27 cotton voile check Designers Guild 28 voile check Designers Guild 29 cotton striped voile Habitat

pages 40–41 30 printed cotton Cath Kidston 31 wool mix felt J.W.Bollom 32 cotton stripe The Blue Door 33 cotton stripe Pukka Palace 34 cotton check Colefax & Fowler 35 cotton check Colefax & Fowler 36 cotton stripe The Blue Door 37 cotton stripe Habitat 38 cotton chambray R. Halstuk 39 linen check The Blue Door 40 cotton ticking Ian Mankin 41 cotton stripe The Blue Door 42 printed floral cotton Manuel Canovas 43 cotton viscose check Manuel

Canovas 44 cotton check The Blue Door 45 cotton stripe The Malabar Cotton Co. 46 cotton stripe Habitat 47 printed cotton stripe Laura Ashley 48 & 49 linen herringbone The Blue Door 50 pink cotton check Ian Mankin 51 green cotton check Ian Mankin 52 & 53 cotton checks Ian Mankin 54 printed cotton floral Jane Churchill 55 linen The Blue Door 56 cotton check Habitat 57 cotton check Designers Guild 58 cotton check Ikea 59 cotton check Habitat 60 cotton check Ian Mankin 61 cotton check Designers Guild 62 cotton check Ian Mankin 63 & 64 cotton checks The Malabar Cotton Co. 65 cotton drill Wolfin Textiles 66 cotton stripe Habitat 67 roller towel Universal Towel Company

pages 42–43 68 cotton mix stripe John Lewis 69 cotton denim Z.Butt Textiles 70 cotton ticking Russell & Chapple71 & 72 cotton Habitat 73 cotton stripe Designers Guild 74 linen Muriel Short 75 cotton calico Wolfin Textiles 76 cotton Pierre Frey 77 cotton check Ian Mankin 78 check Ian Mankin 79 wool tartan Anta 80 wool check Anta 81 cotton Osborne & Little 82 cotton duck Russell & Chapple 83 cotton canvas Wolfin Textiles 84 cotton gingham daisy Sanderson 85 cotton check Designers Guild 86 cotton check Habitat 87

self-patterned cotton/viscose Marvic Textiles 88, 89 & 90 cotton Osborne & Little 91 cotton The Conran Shop 92 cotton check Designers Guild 93 cotton gingham daisy Sanderson 94 cotton check Habitat 95 cotton check Colefax & Fowler 96 linen Wolfin Textiles

pages 44–45 chairs left to right painted in 39-03 salad green eggshell Sanderson Spectrum; covered in floral cotton print Manuel Canovas; painted in 24-04 Swiss blue eggshell Sanderson Spectrum; painted in 21-10 fidelity Sanderson Spectrum

page 46 counter clockwise from top: Bunny chair Designers Guild; pine Lantula dining room table Ikea; junk shop chair, fabric Cath Kidston; folding chair The Reject Shop; factory chair After Noah

page 47 clockwise from top: zinc-top table Cath Kidston; Montecarlo chair The Conran Shop; metal table The Conran Shop; white folding chair Ikea; wooden kitchen table Decorative Living; stool Habitat; peasant beech chair McCord; folding chair The Reject Shop; church chair Castle Gibson; birchwood ply trestle table McCord

page 47 center: table Ikea painted in Color World E5-16 Bromel eggshell, J. W. Bollom

page 48 above: Douglas Fir bed in Pawson House, London, designed by John Pawson; left: four-poster bed frame Ikea; right: wrought iron bed After Noah

page 49 clockwise from top: Coward sofa SCP; Swedish cot sofa Sasha Waddell; armchair George Smith

page 50 kitchen units Ikea

page 51 metal mesh wardrobe Action Handling Equipment; cotton accessory bags Hold Everything, USA; wardrobe junk shop; dresser Colette Aboudaram, France

pages 52–53 Misu glass tumblers Ikea; metal mesh basket Crate & Barrel, USA

page 54 clockwise from top: stainless steel pedal bin Divertimenti; garlic crusher, whisk, crab crackers Divertimenti; glass lemon squeezer Woolworths; kettle Staines Catering

page 55 clockwise from top: Le Pentole steamer Divertimenti; Le Creuset pot, Divertimenti; fish kettle Gill Wing; colander Woolworths; espresso maker McCord; cutlery McCord; corkscrew Divertimenti; scissors John Lewis; Sabatier stainless steel

knife Divertimenti; grater Divertimenti; strainer Divertimenti; Le Pentole frying pan Divertimenti

page 56 clockwise from top: candle holder Habitat; pendant light After Noah; nightlights Ikea; lantern Habitat

page 57 anglepoise lamp After Noah

page 58 galvanized steel storage boxes Muji; shoe rack Ikea; clothes rail B.S. Sales

page 59 clockwise from top: buckets The Conran Shop and hardware stores; butchers hooks Divertimenti; glass storage jars Divertimenti; laundry basket Tobias and the Angel; blue and green cotton fabric The Conran Shop; blanket Melin Tregwynt; beaker Muji; shoe boxes fabric Manuel Canovas; J. W. Bollom; peg rail Ikea

page 60 shadow boxes Habitat

page 61 pudding basins Divertimenti; picture frames Habitat

page 62 clockwise from top: cream cup and saucer by Veronique Pichon at Designers Guild; Poole pottery jug Designers Guild; Champagne flute The Conran Shop; Duralex tumbler Spanish supermarket; ripple glass Designers Guild; tumbler Crate & Barrel, USA; tumbler Pottery Barn, USA; Misu tumbler Ikea; mug Habitat; white coffee cup and saucer

Habitat; blue-and-white china Crate & Barrel, USA

page 63 clockwise from top: tartan plate Anta; Cornishware plate Heal's gingham bowl McCord; blue-and-white bowl Habitat; spotty bowl Designers Guild; jug Divertimenti; white plate Wedgwood

pages 66–67 enamel jug Ruby Beets Antiques, USA

pages 68–69 saucepans Brick Lane Market; tartan plates Anta; sink and taps Aston Matthews

pages 70–71 Swedish stove Jotul; interior design Susie Manby

pages 72–73 Kilner jars After Noah; cake tins Brick Lane Market; white metal chair Brimfield Market USA

pages 74–75 chair cover fabric similar at Universal Towel Company; white bowls from a selection at Wolfman Gold & Good Co., USA

page 76 Provençal chairs Paris junk shop

page 77 above: table and chairs similar at After Noah; flower pots Clifton Nurseries; white china Gill Wing

page 78 white plates Wedgwood

page 79 chair cover fabric Russell & Chapple; metal table The Conran Shop; curtain fabric Designers Guild; lilac paint Sanderson spectrum vinyl matt emulsion Fascination 2309M pages 80–81 left: wicker parlour chairs Palecek; myrtle topiary Christian Tortu at Takashimaya; white table junk shop; right: laminated Saarinen table and Tulip chair Frank Lord

pages 82–83 above left: loft dining area by James Lynch; below left and right: room and furniture in Pawson House, London, designed by John Pawson

pages 84–85 blind fabric Colefax & Fowler; plastic tablecloth John Lewis; wool throw Anta; chandelier Robert Davies; wall paint Country Cream Dulux

pages 86–87 sofa fabric Sanderson; green cotton check pillow Laura Ashley; pillow in blue cotton The Conran Shop; pillows in blue check JAB; throw Anta

pages 88–89 fabric swatches: narrow and wide cotton stripes Habitat; cotton check The Conran Shop; main picture: floral cotton covers, striped cotton blinds, linen and cotton rug Ralph Lauren, USA; ticking pillow fabric Ralph Lauren, USA and antique samples; right: metal daybed Colette Aboudaram, France; antique ticking on pillow fabric Bryony Thomasson

page 90 blue cotton sofa fabric The Conran Shop, Paris; terracotta cotton armchair fabric Ian Mankin; interior design by Susie Manby

page 91 above: paint Olive and Calke Green matt emulsion mixed together Farrow & Ball, candle holder and side cupboard After Noah; main picture: chair and sofa cover, cotton rug and paint Ralph Lauren, USA; pillow cover fabric Designers Guild

pages 92–93 main picture: blinds in checked cotton Designers Guild; wing chair covered in Tulipan Marvic textiles; cream paint Buttermilk Dulux; white table Brick Lane market; right: checked terracotta fabric on sofa Manuel Canovas; wooden chest and metal planter Tobias and The Angel; Butler's tray table Crate & Barrel, USA, painted in Sanderson Spectrum Satinwood 50-23

page 94 light Lieux, Paris; wool appliqué cover Siécle, Paris

page 95 left: basket chair Alfies Antique Market; mirror from Cligoncourt Market, Paris; right: wall paint color Nantucket, Benjamin Moore USA

pages 96–97 main picture: wool blankets Anta; cotton rugs Habitat; cupboard Ikea; checked cotton chair covers Ian Mankin; chairs A Barn Full of Sofas and Chairs; chandelier Wilchester County; shades The Dining Room Shop

page 98 chair in antique ticking Bryony Thomasson; interior design Susie Manby

page 99 filing cabinet B.S. Sales; trestle table McCord; filing boxes, frames Ikea; metal chair and cover in cotton check Habitat; Bunny chair Designers Guild; wastepaper basket The Conran Shop; sofa Ikea

page 100 below: curtain fabric The Conran Shop

page 101 linen curtain fabric from a selection Rosebrand Textiles, USA; myrtle tree Christian Tortu at Takashimaya, New York; sofa from a barn sale; wall paint Nantucket Benjamin Moore, USA

page 104 bed Portobello Road Market; chair Alfies Antique Market; white paint John Oliver

page 105 old linen Judy Greenwood

page 106 table Colette Aboudaram, France

page 107 striped cotton pillowcase Ralph Lauren, USA; patchwork quilt on bed Ruby Beets Antiques, USA; quilt on wall, Brimfield Market, USA

page 108 Tom Dixon light Gladys Mougin, Paris; Indian cotton bedspread Living Tradition, Paris

page 109 mosquito net Mombasa Net Canopies, USA

page 110 bed Jim Howitt; antique quilt Judy Greenwood; pillowcases in cotton lawn Liberty; linen fabric on seat pillows Laura Ashley; white bedlinen John Lewis; paint Dulux Sandstone eggshell

page 111 bolster pad John Lewis; cotton striped fabric Laura Ashley; wooden box Tobias and The Angel

page 112 muslin curtains Pottery Barn, USA; bedlinen Designers Guild; wool blanket Melin Tregwynt

page 113 bunkbeds Habitat Paris

page 116 above: shower curtain similar at Crate & Barrel, USA; below left: drawstring bag fabric Russell & Chapple; starfish Eaton Shell Shop

page 117 antique cupboard Colette Aboudaram, France; interior design Susie Manby

page 118 wooden duckboard Habitat

page 119 above left: peg rail Robert Davies chair Alfies Antique Market; above right: linen basket Habitat top; below: shoe rack, pine mirror, butcher's hooks After Noah; brushes, soaps The Conran

Shop; towels Muji; galvanized bucket The Conran Shop; medicine bottles junk shop

page 120 jug from a selection at Sage Street Antiques, USA; peg rail Ikea

page 121 taps and bath Lassco; wooden bath rack Habitat; towels John Lewis

page 122 nail brush John Lewis; below: tap and stone basin in Pawson House, London, designed by John Pawson

page 123 main picture: taps and bath Lassco; bath rack Habitat; right: outdoor brass taps from builders' merchants

page 124 bathroom by James Lynch; bath Lassco; shower taps Nicholls and Clarke; tins Alfies Antique Market

page 125 left: towels, flannels and robe Designers Guild; right: towels John Lewis

pages 126–127 cutlery Designers Guild; beaker Heal's; blanket Anta; table Brick Lane Market

page 129 tablecloth fabric Designers Guild; chair and table Clifton Nurseries

page 130–131 beakers Heal's; tablecloth fabric and pillows Designers Guild

Please note that credits were correct at time of photography but availability of items may have changed.

suppliers

home

ABC Carpet & Home
881–888 Broadway
New York, NY 10003
tel: 212-674-1144
www.abchome.com
Exotic collection of home furnishings, fabrics, carpets, and design accessories.

Bed, Bath & Beyond
620 Sixth Avenue
New York, NY 10011
tel: 212-255-3550
www.bedbathandbeyond.com
Everything for the bedroom and bathroom, plus kitchen utensils, home décor, and storage solutions.

Crate & Barrel
650 Madison Avenue
New York, NY 10022
tel: 212-308-0011
www.crateandbarrel.com
A wonderful source of good value furniture and accessories, from simple white china and glass, to chairs and beds.

Fishs Eddy
889 Broadway
New York, NY 10011
tel: 212-420-2090
www.fishseddy.com
Supplies of great Fifties-style china mugs, bowls, etc.

Garnet Hill
231 Main Street
Franconia, NH 03580
www.garnethill.com
*Bedlinen in natural fibers,
wonderful down duvets
and pillows.*

Hold Everything
1311 Second Avenue
New York, NY 10021
tel: 212-879-1450
www.holdeverything.com
*Everything for storage from
baskets to bookshelves.*

IKEA
1800 East McConnor
Parkway
Schaumburg, IL 60173
www.ikea.com
*Home basics at great prices,
including assembly kit
furniture, stylish,
inexpensive kitchenware.*

Palecek
The Design Pavilion #209
200 Kansas Street
San Francisco, CA 94103
tel: 800-274-7730
www.palecek.com
*Manufacturers of painted
wicker furniture.*

Pier One Imports
71 Fifth Avenue
New York, NY 10003
tel: 212-206-1911
www.pier1.com
*Great home accessories,
furniture and outdoor ideas.*

Portico Bed & Bath
72 Spring Street
New York, NY 10012
tel: 212-941-7800
www.porticohome.com
*Beautiful white linens, plus
towels and throws.*

Pottery Barn
600 Broadway
New York, NY 10012
tel: 212-219-2420
www.potterybarn.com
*Everything from furniture to
decoration details, such as
muslin curtains, china,
pillows, and candlesticks.*

Restoration Hardware
935 Broadway
New York, NY 10011
tel: 212-260-9479
www.restorationhardware.
com
*Not just hardware, some of
the funkiest home
furnishings, lighting and
home and garden
accessories you'll find.*

Takashimaya
693 Fifth Avenue
New York, NY 10012
tel: 212-350-0100
*Exquisite and exclusive
bedlinen, soaps, and
lotions. Includes Christian
Tortu florist at front of
shop, with heavenly fresh
cut flowers, topiary trees,
and delicious scented
candles.*

Waverly
www.waverly.com
*Complete supply of
decorative accessories
including fabric, wallpaper,
furniture, window
treatments, tabletop, paint,
and floor coverings.*

Williamsburg
Marketplace Catalogue
The Colonial Williamsburg
Foundation
Department 023
P.O. Box 3532
Williamsburg, VA 23187
tel: 800-414-6291
www.williamsburgmarket
place.com
*Historically accurate home
furnishings, prints, and
keepsakes.*

Williams-Sonoma
121 East 59th Street
New York, NY 10022
tel: 917-369-1131
www.williams-sonoma.com
*Cooking utensils, fine
linens, and classic china.*

fabrics

Laura Ashley Home Store
171 East Ridgewood Avenue
Ridgewood, NJ 07450
tel: 201-670-0686
www.lauraashley.com
Floral, striped, checked, and solid cottons in a wide variety of colors.

Calvin Klein Home
At Calvin Klein
645 Madison Avenue
New York, NY 10021
tel: 212-292-9000
Classic collection of linens and blankets.

Fabrics To Dye For
67 Tom Harvey Road
Westerly
Rhode Island, 02891
tel: 401-348-6000
www.fabricstodyefor.com
Hand-painted fabrics, dyes, and kits, also available at a variety of retail locations.

Hancock Fabrics
2605A West Main Street
Tupelo, MS 38801
tel: 662-844-7368
www.hancockfabrics.com
America's largest fabric store, good for all basic decoration needs.

On Board Fabrics
Route 27, P.O. Box 14
Edgecomb, ME 04556
tel: 207-882-7536
www.onboardfabrics.com
From Balinese cottons to Italian tapestry, botanical prints and woven plaids.

Salsa Fabrics
3100 Holly Avenue
Silver Springs, NV 89429
tel: 775-577-2207
www.salsafabrics.com
Great original fabrics in cotton, silk, and wool from Guatemala and Indonesia.

food

Balducci's
424 Sixth Avenue
New York, NY 10012
tel: 212-673-2600
Fine Italian delicacies and prepared foods by mail order.

Dean & Deluca
560 Broadway
New York, NY 10012
tel: 212-226-6800
www.deananddeluca.com
A foodhall and kitchen-ware store of epic proportions with everything from wild mushrooms to coffee, including imported gourmet fare.

Hometown Favorites, Inc.
tel: 888-694-2656
www.hometownfavorites.com
Unique food shop stocking over 400 hard-to-find old-time favorites like Bea's Dilled Green Tomatoes, Cincinnati Style Dixie Chili, Stegner's Mock Turtle Soup, and Quaker Quisp Cereal.

modern furniture

B & B Italia USA
150 East 58th Street
New York, NY 10155
tel: 800-872-1697
www.bebitalia.it
Specializes in Bellini, Cittero, Pesce, Scarpa, and others.

Design Within Reach
455 Jackson Street
San Francisco, CA 94111
tel: 415-837-3940
www.dwr.com
A consumer-friendly shop supplying furniture from over fifty modern designers including Alessi, Ghery, and Knoll.

Full Upright Position
tel: 800-431-5134
www.fup.com
Stocks furniture designed by Aalto, Eames, Le Corbusier, van der Rohe and more.

MOMA Design Store
44 West 53rd Street
New York, NY 10022
tel: 212-767-1050
www.momastore.org
A finely honed selection of furniture, lighting, kitchen, and tabletop accessories by modern designers including Stark, Wright, and Vasa.

Workbench
Flagship location:
470 Park Avenue South
New York, NY 10016
tel: 212-481-5454
www.workbenchfurniture.com

Clean and functional
imported Danish furniture
for bedrooms, dining and
living rooms.

paints

Janovic
1150 Third Avenue
New York, NY 10021
tel: 212-772-1400
www.janovic.com
*A quality selection of paints
in a wide color range.*

Ralph Lauren Paint Collection
At Ralph Lauren
867 Madison Avenue
New York, NY 10021
tel: 212-606-2100
www.rlhome.polo.com
*Signature collection of
colors grouped in romantic
themes such as River Rock
and Desert Hollywood.*

Benjamin Moore Paints
Product Information Center:
51 Chestnut Ridge Road
Montvale, NJ 07645
www.benjaminmooore.com
*A spectrum of over 1,400
colors, including muted
shades and period styles.*

Martha Stewart Paint Collection
At Kmart
tel: 888-627-8429
www.kmart.com
*A quality selection of
decorator shades inspired
by Martha's Auracana
chickens.*

secondhand and antiques

Ruby Beets Antiques
Poxybogue Road
Bridgehampton, NY 11932
tel: 516-537-2802
*Painted furniture, old white
china, and kitchenware.*

Victor DiPaola Antiques
Long Island, NY
tel: 516-488-5868
www.dipaolaantiques.com
*Furniture and decorative
arts of the 18th and 19th
centuries.*

English Country Antiques
Snake Hollow Road
Bridgehampton, NY 11932
tel: 516-537-0606
*Period country furniture in
pine, plus decorative blue-
and-white china.*

Tri-State Antique Center
47 West Pike
Canonsburg, PA 15317
tel: 724-745-9116
tristateantiques.com
*Specializes in Heywood-
Wakefield, Mid-Century
Modern furniture, and
pottery, china, and glass.*

Up The Creek's
American Antique Furniture
Market
209 North Tower
Centralia, WA 98531
tel: 360-330-0427
www.amerantfurn.com
*American antique furniture
and lighting in Victorian,
Eastlake, Turn-of-the
century, Mission, Arts &
Crafts, Depression and
1940s' Classic Revival
periods in both restored
and original finish.*

*A listing of over 40,000
addresses of Antiques
Shops throughout the
country exists at
www.curioscape.com.*

Flea Markets
Brimfield Antique Show
Route 20
Brimfield, MA 01010
tel: 413-245-3436
www.brimfieldshow.com
*Renowned as the Outdoor
Antiques Capital of the
World, this show is held for
a week in the months of
May, July, and September.*

*For listings of flea markets
held throughout the
country, go to
www.fleamarketguide.com.*

index

a

alcoves 41
aluminium 47, 59, 99
armchairs 49
armoires 109

b

bags 8, 116
barbecues 78
basins 8, 25, 61, 123
baskets 8, 27, 30, 50, 59, 60, 102, 111, 119, 125, 126, 130
bath cabinets 118
bath racks 115
bathmats 115, 118, 119
bathrooms 9, 20, 28, 38, 114–25
baths 28, 116, 118, 119–20
bedlinen 9, 12, 15, 27, 48, 105, 106, 107, 108, 111, 112, 113
bedrooms 20, 38, 102–13
beds 9, 48, 105, 111
bateau 108
bunk 111, 112
    cast-iron 48
    divan 48
    four-poster 48, 111
    streamlined 48

bedspreads 109
bedsteads 105, 111
beechwood 46, 47, 70
benches 82
blankets 9, 27, 48, 59, 102, 105, 107, 113
blinds 21, 38, 41, 42, 84, 88, 90, 100, 102
boilers 125
bolster covers 42
bolster pillows 41
bolsters 88, 111
bookcases 45
bottles 29, 53, 124
bowls 16, 34, 53, 61, 63, 74, 79, 84, 92
bows 41, 93
box skirts 93
boxes 22, 58, 59, 60, 73, 102, 111, 119, 125
brooms 53, 54
brushes 21, 31, 115, 125
buckets 21, 58, 59, 78, 96, 118
bump 100
bunk beds 111, 112
butler's trays 92
button detailing 41, 93

c

candelabra 81, 119
candlelight 9, 56, 84, 119
candles 8, 34, 56, 66, 74, 84, 87, 129
cane 119
canvas 36, 42, 100, 129
carpets 27, 97, 123
casseroles 55
chair covers 17, 19, 20, 22, 41
chairs 41, 90, 96
    architect's 45

basket 94
butterfly 46
café 47
church 46, 47
dining 42, 45, 77
factory 46
fold-up 46, 81, 129, 130
kitchen 45, 81
ladderback 82
mismatched 98
office 82
rush-seated 46, 47
slatted 46, 47, 130
Tulip 82
chandeliers 56, 77, 84, 96
checks 8, 16, 25, 41, 49, 59, 63, 72, 74, 84, 88, 90, 92, 97, 129
cheese 9, 126, 129
chesterfields 90
chests of drawers 111
china 12, 15, 17, 25, 60, 62, 63, 72, 73, 74, 76
Christmas 77–78
citrus fruit squeezers 54
clothes rods 58
coir 22, 30, 97
colanders 55
color 12–24
    beige 22
    blues 8, 16–17, 65, 84, 91, 95, 122, 124
    brown 12, 20
    chocolate 22
    cream 12, 22, 24, 25, 65, 84, 94, 106
    earth 22–23
    gray 91, 94, 96, 107
    green 8, 12, 18–19, 65, 84, 91, 106, 122, 124

lavender 20–21, 65, 95
neutral 12, 94
orange 25
pink 12, 20–21, 95, 106
terra-cotta 22–23, 92
whites 8, 12, 14–15, 25, 65, 94, 95, 106
yellow 8, 12, 24–25, 84, 106
computer hardware 27
concrete 31
cookers 72, 73
cool boxes 129
corkscrews 54, 55
cotton 8, 9, 12, 16, 17, 19, 20, 25, 27, 31, 36, 38, 41, 42, 46, 49, 59, 74, 79, 81, 84, 87, 88, 90, 91, 93, 95, 97–100, 102, 107, 113, 116, 130
cotton denim 42
cotton drill 15
cotton lace 113
cotton lawn 38, 111
creamware 62, 63
crockery 25
cupboards 9, 51, 61, 68, 70, 73, 84, 125
cups 62, 63, 79
curtain poles 100, 100
curtains 16, 22, 41, 79, 87, 88, 95, 99, 100, 111
half 38
unlined 100
cutlery 55, 59, 74

d

David, Elizabeth: *Summer Cooking* 129
daybeds 41, 49, 88, 111
denim 12, 16, 17, 42, 107

dining areas/rooms 41, 56, 69, 74–85
dishwashers 70
display 60–61, 72
distemper 31
domette 100
doors
 cupboard 73
 panelled 31, 102
downlighters 56
drapes 15, 38, 41, 42, 88, 100
drawers 50, 68
dressers 50, 73
duck 42
duckboards 115
duvet covers 38
duvets 102, 113

e

eating outdoors 126, 128–30
electric juicers 70
embroidery 105
emulsion 15, 79, 91
espresso makers 54, 55

f

fabrics 8, 9, 27, 36–43
 durable 42–43
 light 38–39
 versatile 40–41
faucets 115, 123, 124
filing cabinets 45, 99
fireplaces 82, 84
fires 9, 87, 93
fish 9, 130
fish kettles 55
flags 22, 28
floorboards 15, 28, 91, 111
flooring 22, 27, 30, 72, 91, 94, 97, 98, 99, 108, 118, 123

flower pots 16, 81, 84
flowers 8, 9, 22, 25, 34, 66, 74, 78, 84, 92, 106
fruit 9
fry pans 55
furniture 44–51, 65
 beds 48
 bentwood 108
 cupboards and storage 50–51
 painted 15
 sofas and seating 49
 tables and chairs 46–47

g

garden borders 12, 20
garlic crushers 54
glass 17, 29, 62, 66, 74, 76, 84, 107, 124
graters 55

h

herbs 78, 129, 130
home study 99
hurricane shades 56
hyacinths 78

i

ice cream 130

j

Jacobsen, Arne 46
jam jars 58
jars 8, 9, 58, 59, 61, 66, 74, 129
jugs 63, 78, 92, 106, 120

k

kelims 16, 92
kettles 54
kitchens 25, 28, 34, 66, 68–73
knives 54, 55

l

ladles 73
lamps 56, 92
lanterns 56
larder cupboards 73
laundry baskets 111, 119
lavatories 123
lighting 56–57, 99, 106
lights
    desk 53, 56, 99
    pendant 56
limestone 82
linen 9, 22, 36, 41, 42, 49, 66, 74, 87, 90, 99, 100, 109, 111, 113
linoleum 118, 123
living rooms 86–101
lobster crackers 54
loft-style living spaces 31
log baskets 8, 27, 98
logs 27, 84, 93
loofahs 115
loose covers 17, 38, 42, 46, 49, 81, 88, 90, 93, 96

m

mantelpieces 92
maple 70
marble 28, 66, 70, 92
Mason jars 8, 58
matting 22, 94, 97
mattress covers 41
mattresses 9, 102, 111, 113
meat hooks 58, 59

medicine cabinets 118
microwaves 70
mirrors 94
mosaic 124
mosquito nets 108
mugs 8, 21, 60, 62, 73
muslin 9, 15, 21, 36, 42, 81, 99, 100, 102, 109, 111, 112

n

napkins 38, 74, 77
natural fiber 22
nightlights 56

o

oak 82
objects 52–63
china and glass 62–63
display 60–61
lighting 56–57
storage 58–59
utensils 54–55
organdy 100
outdoor living 126–31
oyster knives 55

p

pans 28, 60, 70, 73
paper
silver 29
tissue 28
waxed 28–29
parquet 91, 108
pebbles 8, 29, 60
peg rails 120
photographs 60
picnics 126, 128, 129
pillow cases 38, 105, 106, 107, 111
pillows/pillow covers 12, 15, 17, 19, 20, 27, 36, 38, 89,

41, 42, 84, 87, 88, 91, 95, 102, 113, 130,
pinewood 46, 47, 48, 73, 82, 94, 112
piping 41
plaster 31
plastic 21
plate drainers 73
plates 9, 63, 66, 76, 79, 84
pleats 41, 93
plywood 70
pot pourri 34
pots 28, 59, 60, 70, 73, 78
    clay 22, 92
    flower 16, 81, 84
prints 61, 120
pumice stones 27, 31

q

quilts 9, 21, 102, 106, 107, 111

r

refrigerators 54
roller blinds 38, 100
roller towels 74, 81
Roman blinds/drapes 21, 41, 42, 84, 88, 100
rugs 92, 97, 106, 126
rush 46, 47

s

saucepans 53
saucers 62
scents 8, 32, 116
school lockers 119
scissors 54, 55
seagrass 97
Shaker style 16, 48, 59, 111
sheeting 8, 38, 77, 82, 93, 102, 105, 106, 113

shells 8, 27, 60, 61, 70
shelving 51, 72, 73, 84, 109, 120
shoe racks 58
shower stalls 123
showers 115, 116, 124, 124
sideboards 84
silk 36
sinks 70, 73, 116, 122, 123
sisal 30, 94, 97
sitting/living rooms 20, 41, 86–101
skirting 91
slate 28, 66
slipcovers 15, 20, 42, 46, 49, 81, 88, 89, 90, 91, 96, 98
soaps 8, 9, 28, 115, 116
sofas 20, 42, 45, 49, 88, 90, 96
sponges 115, 116, 125
spongeware 62
spoons 28, 54, 59
stainless-steel 28, 54, 55, 66, 82, 123
steamers 55
stools 47, 92
storage 50, 51, 58–59, 66, 73, 84, 102, 109, 119, 125
stoves 54, 69
strainers 53, 54, 55, 73
stripes 8, 16, 17, 19, 41, 74, 88, 91, 95, 97, 107, 129

t

table runners 74
table settings 74, 77
tablecloths 38, 41, 66, 72, 74, 77, 79, 84, 95, 130, 130
tables 46
    bedside 107
    dining 47, 82
    fold-up 45, 130

formica-topped 118
pattern-cutting 45
pine 47
refectory 81
side 84
trestle 46, 47, 78, 82, 99, 130
zinc-topped 47
tartan 17, 42, 97
tartanware 63
taste 8, 32, 34
teak 70
terra-cotta 16, 30, 81, 91, 123
texture 8, 21, 26–31, 65, 98
    rough 30–31
    smooth 28–29
throws 88, 91, 93, 98
ticking 17, 41, 87, 88, 95, 99, 111
tiling 28, 30, 72, 91, 116, 120, 123, 124
tins 72, 73
tongue-and-groove 31, 120
towel rails 119
towels 9, 31, 116, 124, 125
toy storage 58, 59
trash cans 54
trolleys 73
trunks 111
tumblers 74, 130

u

umbrellas, canvas 129
underfloor heating 93

v

varnish 15
vases 63, 77, 78
vegetables 9, 59
viscose 42
voile 38

w

walls
    brickwork 91
    concrete 31
    painted 15, 16, 20, 25, 31, , 84, 89, 106, 107, 116
    panelled 111
    tiled 28, 116
wardrobes 50, 51, 102, 109
washbasins 120
whisks 54, 73
window treatments 38, 100, 106
windows
    attic 41
    sash 100
wine glasses 74, 76
wood 66, 82
see also individual woods
wool 9, 27, 36, 42, 49, 87, 97, 98, 105, 107, 113
work surfaces 28, 70, 73
wreaths 8, 92

y

yacht varnish 15

z

zinc 47, 82, 99, 111

acknowledgments

I want to say a huge thank you to Jacqui Small, Anne Ryland, David Peters, Sian Parkhouse, Sophie Pearse, Penny Stock, Janet Cato, and everyone at RPS, who have worked like Trojans to produce *Pure Style*.

I am indebted to Henry Bourne, whose stunning photographs have captured the spirit of the book so perfectly.

I would also like to thank Nick Pope for the excellent cut-out photography.

Many, many thanks to my assistant Fiona Craig-McFeely, who has been an invaluable source of efficiency and support.

Thanks to Tessa Brown for making up the soft furnishing projects.

I would like to thank the following people for allowing us to photograph their homes for inclusion in *Pure Style*: Shiraz Maneksha; Ilse Crawford; James Lynch and Sian Tucker; John and Catherine Pawson, Pawson House, London; Marie Kalt; John and Claudia Brown; Peri Wolfman and Charles Gold, Wolfman Gold & Good Co.; Tricia Foley; Ellen O'Neill; Mary Emmerling; Gary Wright, and Sheila Teague.

My family have been unfailingly supportive, and have put up with many months of upheaval. Big hugs for my husband Alastair, my children Tom, Georgia, and Grace, and my mother and father.